Nesting

Nesting:
body
dwelling
mind

S A R A H   R O B I N S O N

William Stout Publishers
1326-1328 S. 51st Street
Richmond, CA 94804
www.stoutpublishers.com

Design by Sylvie Astrid
Editing by Jennifer Sime

ISBN: 978-0-9819667-1-7
LCCN: 2011930148

Printed in China

To my family

Nesting: body, dwelling, mind

ACKNOWLEDGEMENTS

I am convinced that what we end up doing in life is not so much a conscious choice as it is a surrender to the inevitable. I started out studying philosophy because I couldn't stop asking "Why?" I pursued architecture because it seemed so practical, but the questions persisted. The French philosopher Gaston Bachelard addressed the question of why architecture matters through studying birds' nests and shells. This book is a humble homage to him.

The revolution taking place in the sciences of the mind has astonishing implications for the practice of architecture. This book follows Bachelard's prophetic inquiry by using the findings of the cognitive and brain sciences to understand how architecture shapes us and why it matters. I am fully aware that this is an audacious enterprise. I write this as a practicing architect who is certain to miss the nuances and distinctions involved in the work of many lifetimes. It is because of the importance of this new body of scientific knowledge that I have risked overstepping my bounds. So, I wish to thank you, the reader, for embarking on this journey with me.

Juhani Pallasmaa's kindness, integrity, and generosity were an immeasurable support to this work. I would like to extend my gratitude to William Stout, for his patience, Jennifer Sime, for her attentive eye, David Mohney, for his encouragement, Roxanne Davis, dear friend and writing comrade, and my husband, Paolo Bazzurro, who never doubted me even for a moment.

S.R.

THE HUMAN NEST

Juhani Pallasmaa

In the fusion of place and soul, the soul is as much of a container of place as place is a container of soul, and both are susceptible to the same forces of destruction.

– Robert Pogue Harrison

We cannot mentally survive in a placeless, scaleless and meaningless physical space. We inhabit our physical world through structuring it into mental space; by turning infinite and uniform natural space into distinct places and giving these places specific cultural and mental meanings. We are likewise unable to live in measureless natural time as we need to give our experiential time its human scale.

The most significant means of transforming natural space and time into cultural and mental meanings is architecture. As philosopher Karsten Harries states, "Architecture is not only about domesticating space. It is also a deep defense against the terror of time. The language of beauty is essentially the language of timeless reality."[1] This transformation takes place mostly on an unconscious level through a silent pre-understanding that provides a horizon for experience and the arising of meaning. The fusion of self and setting is so complete that we tend to become blind to the characteristics and qualities of our environments. We tend to think of meaning as something that is symbolic and linguistically expressed, but architectural meanings are fundamentally lived existential and embodied experiences that are imbedded in specific spatial situations of which we are not normally aware. As Jean-Paul Sartre states, "Understanding is not a quality coming to human reality from outside, it is its characteristic way of existing."[2]

Gaston Bachelard objects to the idea of a primary human anxiety arising from being thrown into the world as, in his view, we are born in the cradle of architecture.[3] This cradle mediates between us and the world, giving our experiences of the world specific meanings from the very onset of our awareness. Our house is the mysterious point Omega described by Teilhard de Chardin, from which the world appears complete and right.[4] We are born into a world which has already been culturally domesticated by human constructions, both material and mental. Our house is both our cradle and our nest in the world.

The notion of nest implies intimacy and familiarity. The nest is a direct projection and product of the body, its movements and its rest, and it is the most perfect of dwellings. In *The Poetics of Space* Bachelard has included a chapter on nests. To point out the perfection of the bird nest he quotes Ambroise Paré: "The enterprise and skill with which animals make their nests is so efficient that it is not possible to do better, so entirely do they surpass all masons, carpenters and builders, for there is not a man who would be able to make a house better suited to himself and to his children than these little animals build for themselves. This is so true, in fact, that we have a proverb according to which men can do everything except build a bird's nest."[5]

We tend to regard bird, animal, and insect nests as charming curiosities of animal building behaviour. Yet, even a cursory study of the subject reveals astonishing functional, behavioural, and technical refinements in their processes of construction and functional performance. Animal constructions are perfect responses to the specific patterns of life of the species in question. We can rate numerous animal structures as more refined constructions than any human architecture. In fact, Edward O. Wilson, the pioneer of biophilia, the science and ethics of the love of life, considers the nest of the leaf-cutter ant and the ant's processes of survival a more complex system than any invention of humankind.[6] In addition to their functional efficiency, animal nests are usually also stunningly beautiful. No wonder Joseph Brodsky, the poet, claims, "The purpose of evolution, believe it or not, is beauty."[7]

Countless human vernacular cultures have perfected their buildings similarly through repeated trial and error, a principle built into all natural systems of selection. Human technological cultures, on the other hand, have distanced, or "emancipated", their building processes from their connections with the body and the guiding processes of the biological world. In our obsessive separation of the material and mental worlds, body and mind, emotion and reason, we have cut our dependency on the internal principles of nature that work for balance, perfection, and beauty.

The nest protects and supports the body, but it also centers and organizes the occupant's world; the world gathers and structures itself around the nest. The intimacy and hapticity of the nest project erotic connotations as suggested by the notion "love nest". The most intimate spatial experiences are sensations of the skin; we feel the caressing embrace of space and even light acquires tangible and haptic qualities. The deepest experience of the intimacy and protectiveness of home is an unconscious experience of naked skin. Bach-elard points out the fundamentally embodied and haptic manner of dwelling: "To curl up belongs to the phenomenology of the verb to inhabit, and only those who have learned to do so can inhabit with intensity."[8]

Profound architecture responds equally to the requirements of the body and the mind. In fact, our difficulties in grasping the essence of the human condition arise from the separation of these two realms. As recent neurological research has revealed, the mind is fundamentally embodied. The life-supporting and sensitive house resonates with the body and even predicts its movements and desires. It opens up a window into the wall exactly at the point where we wish to look out and see the garden, and it presents the first step of the stair on the instance that we have a desire to go upstairs. The responsive house offers a seat exactly when we wish to sit down, and a protected corner when we want to withdraw and be alone. Profound architecture choreographs the acts, events and movements of daily life; we can appropriately speak of spatial and architectural choreography and scores.

At the same time, a responsive building anticipates our emotions and mental expectations. It provides light and shadow, enclosure and view, solitude and participation, quietude and sound, intimacy and openness, in accordance with the dweller's mental and emotive dynamics. It also orchestrates experiences of seasons, hours of the day, as well as changes of weather for the dweller's enjoyment. As the house mediates between the world and the dweller, it becomes part of his or her extended skin and surface of interaction with the world. The house is a mental device and filter as much as it is a protection for our fragile bodies. It houses our dreams and fantasies, memories and desires, fears and wishes in addition to facilitating the physical acts of dwelling. Dwelling is an exchange and fusion; as I settle in a space, the space settles in me and it turns into an ingredient of my sense of self. "I am the space, where I am," as Noël Arnaud, the poet, states.[9] Or, as Maurice Merleau-Ponty puts it, "The world is wholly inside, and I am wholly outside myself."[10] Rainer Maria Rilke uses the touching notion *Weltinnenraum*, the interior space of the world for the experience of profound belonging.[11]

Human constructions, agricultural fields and gardens, roads and bridges, cities and villages, institutions and dwellings, rooms and corners, give a structured articulation and meaning to our experiences of the world. We even structure the natural landscape through the act of naming its various characteristics and phenomenal features: mountain, valley, grove, and the comfort offered in the shadow of a tree.

Western industrial culture has a frustrated and dualistic attitude towards the human body. On the one hand, the body is revered as the object of social and sexual identity and appeal, on the other, its fundamental role in experience, consciousness, and cognition continues to be unrecognised and underrated. Maurice Merleau-Ponty uses the notions "chiasm" and "intertwining" to denote the inseparable bind between the self and the world.[12] Like the magical Moebius strip which has only one surface, the world and the self constitute one entity that appears to consist of two polarities, but in fact constitutes a singularity; the self slides unnoticeably into the world and vice versa. In a similar fashion the body and the mind constitute the singularity of self.

The quickly emerging requirement for ecological ethics and sustainable architectural rationality is surely the most important force of change in architecture since the breakthrough of modernity a cen-

tury ago. The challenge calls for a new understanding of form and performance, artistic objectives and scientific understanding, aesthetics and ethics, and indeed ourselves as bio-cultural and historical beings.

We architects are used to thinking in terms of space and material form; we think of objects rather than systems, aesthetics rather than processes, the present rather than a temporal continuum. George Lakoff and Mark Johnson have convincingly shown in their book, *The Metaphors We Live By,* that language and thought are fundamentally metaphorical: "Metaphor is pervasive in everyday life, not just in language but in thought and action. Our ordinary conceptual system, in terms of which we both think and act, is fundamentally metaphorical in nature."[13] Arnold H. Modell, the psychiatrist, uses the notion "the biology of meaning" and argues that we are not even aware of the metaphors that guide our thought. He writes, "Metaphor is primarily a form of cognition rather than a trope or figure of speech. Further, metaphor as a cognitive tool can operate unconsciously, so that a metaphoric process is one aspect of the unconscious mind."[14]

Architectural thinking is also engaged in metaphors; in fact we can regard buildings as embodied and lived metaphors of the world. The guiding metaphors of building have shifted from images of shelter to mechanistic ideals, and further to today's refined models of invisible electric and electronic performance. In fact, the current globalized architecture of alluring and memorable images has often flattened architecture into a three-dimensional picture, a spatialized advertisement, as it were.

It is most likely that the future models and metaphors of thought and design—from technology to computers, material sciences, economics, and medicine—will be based on biological imagery, the incredibly refined biological systems of interaction and dynamic balance. This approach, inspired by systems of biological performance, has already emerged in such areas as bionics, biomimicry, and biophilia. So far, these notions have been presented merely as catchwords of a new orientation. Yet the argument by Wilson on the complexity and refinement of the leafcutter ant nest, quoted above, should convince anyone that biological models offer inspiring and challenging metaphors for the refinement of human artifacts and systems.

Also, recent research in neurobiology promises a new understanding of our own neural and brain activities as well as the meaning of aesthetic judgement and pleasure. In his pioneering book, *Inner Vision: An Exploration of Art and the Brain*, neurologist Semir Zeki suggests the possibility "of a theory of aesthetics that is biologically based."[15]

Modern architecture has been future-oriented. Yet we are primarily biological beings whose senses, neural systems, and reactions have developed during millions of years. Along with the wisdom brought about by the study of biological models, a deeper understanding of our own biological and cultural historicity is urgently needed. I have used the notion "mental ecology" in order to expand the notion of ecology to the human mental world, as ecology and sustainability cannot be dealt with merely in technical terms.

Sarah Robinson's book, *Nesting: Body, Dwelling, Mind,* opens up thought-provoking, challenging, and poetic views into a more balanced understanding of ourselves, our relationship with the world, as well as our processes of experience, thought, and feeling. This approach reveals a "biology of meaning" and points towards new metaphors and modes of thought in architecture.

Though we dream of an airy intimacy,
Open and free, yet sheltering as a nest
For passing bird, or mouse, or ardent bee,

Of Love where life in all its forms can rest
As wind breathes in the leaves of a tree;
Though we dream of never having a wall against
All that must flow and pass and cannot be caught,

An ever welcoming self that is not fenced,
Yet we are tethered still to another thought;
The unsheltered cannot shelter,
The exposed, exposes others;
The wide open door means nothing if it cannot be closed.

Those who create real havens are not free
Hold fast, maintain, are rooted, dig deep wells,
Whatever haven human love may be,
There is no freedom without sheltering walls.

And when we imagine wings that come and go
What we see is a house
And a wide open window.

– May Sarton

1

OF HAVENS

The Fall of Icarus, Pieter Brueghel

"Open and free yet sheltering as a nest." The poet captures our profound longing with few words. We all want this: an expanse of sky, possibility without barrier and *also* protection, shelter, and enduring love. The drama of each one of our lives stretches magnetically between poles. Earth-bound we dream of wings, we are both house and wide-open window. This contradictory state, the fact that we do not have "freedom without sheltering walls" describes our human condition. Ours is a song of lament, we resent gravity fashioned as we are of mortal clay. Like Icarus in defiance, our artifice built of wax feathers melts. We have flown too close to the sun. Our adolescent inability to accept limitation, our disregard for future consequence is deeply ingrained in our habits of thought. Our culture supports this sense of limitlessness, teaching us that our consumption "helps" the economy, supraliminal media messages bombard us constantly with images of unreality, vast industries are dedicated to creating fictional "needs". Now that the climate crisis is finally accepted as fact, we are told that we can "help" the earth if we buy more stuff, as long as it is green. Such superficiality does not change much except the color of corporate logos.

The very notion that we can "save" the earth reveals the depth of our delusion. Over the course of two millennia we have gradually abstracted ourselves from the rest of life on earth. We fail to understand that we happen to be the latest participants in a vast evolutionary cycle and our fate is linked inseparably with all of life. Indeed, it is we who need saving. "To save," according to the German phenomenologist Martin Heidegger, "really means to set something free in its own essence."[1] If freedom is a wide open door, its strength is contingent upon sturdy hinges whose movement permits the door to close. When sheltered, our essence can unfold. Salvation perhaps, is not freedom *from* limitation, but *through* it.

For over 2000 years, Western thought has equated freedom with an act of the will. In fact Robert Frost's description, "You have freedom when you are easy in your harness," is a more accurate depiction. Shifting our understanding of limitation underlies our potential for renewal. The word *limit* derives from the Latin root *limes*, which means a boundary, an embankment between fields. *Limit* also shares its root with *limen*, which means threshold. Our own language conjures a wealth of associations for limits: a lush green meadow with a fence, the line that divides inside and outside at a doorway, the boundary of consciousness between dreaming and thinking, the way the sun illuminates the earth's curve when it sets. The etymology of the word discloses its own hidden meanings. We act as though we are the shapers and masters of language, said Heidegger, when in fact it is language that masters us. Our own language suggests that a boundary is not oppressive but necessary, it "is not that at which something stops . . . [it] is that from which something begins its essential unfolding."[2]

"This is a universal law," Friedrich Nietzsche proclaimed, "a living thing can be healthy, strong and fruitful only when bounded by a horizon."[3] Our own most immediate horizon is the boundary of our body; it is the locus of our activity, the ground of our experience in the world. Our mind is nested within our body in an intrinsically intertwined relationship. The extent and importance of this intimate bond is a central topic of study in the relatively young field of cognitive science. Cognitive science is an interdisciplinary effort that encompasses the expertise of linguists, computer scientists, philosophers, psychologists, anthropologists, and neuroscientists who study the structures and processes that underpin our perceptions, thinking, and behavior. In a relatively short time, they have made astonishing discoveries that have vast implications for Western thought.

Although their viewpoints are pluralistic, cognitive scientists do agree on some fundamental issues. Their three major discoveries, elucidated by George Lakoff and Mark Johnson in their book, *Philosophy in the Flesh*, are these: "The mind is inherently embodied, thought is mostly unconscious, and abstract concepts are largely metaphorical."[4] These basic findings radically undermine two thousand years of Western thought. Language and cognition arise from structures in our bodies that we share with other animals. Our thoughts are shaped by our bodily interactions in the world, our unconscious, and through metaphors that operate beneath our awareness. Transcendent reason, pure objectivity, and an existence independent of the environment are fictions derived from an obsolete paradigm.

"Our very organism, rather than some absolute external reality, is used as the ground reference for the constructions we make of the world around us and for the construction of the ever present sense of subjectivity that is part and parcel of our experiences," writes neuroscientist Antonio Damasio. "Our most refined thoughts and actions, our greatest joys and deepest sorrows, use the body as a yardstick."[5] The essence of our feelings arises not from some elusive quality attached to an object but from perception through the boundary of our body. Our experience of the world unfolds from this limit. We live not in a world of fixed representations, but of meanings that arise from the contextual interaction of body, mind, and world.

These groundbreaking findings demand not only a new understanding of our philosophy of mind and body. We also need to come to terms with the extent to which our environment, specifically our built environment, shapes our humanity. Winston Churchill's well known saying that we shape our buildings and thereafter they shape us becomes keenly pertinent in light of the findings of the cognitive scientists. Our thoughts and feelings are molded by our interactions within an environment that we ourselves have fashioned. We are indeed, as historian Lewis Mumford has pointed out, our "own supreme artifact."[6] Faced with the reality of the contemporary built landscape, it is quite alarming to realize that at some basic level our buildings are shaping us. They reflect our growing monoculture: unidimensional and largely inhospitable to authentic life. The French proverb says that we may have succeeded in doing everything, but we still cannot build a bird's nest. We have failed at the seemingly humble and immediate task of housing ourselves.

In his 1951 lecture, "Building Dwelling Thinking", Heidegger showed that the English verb *to be* originally meant place-dwelling. To dwell, he said, "signifies the way we human beings are on earth."[7] The word *dwell* derives from the Greek *homois*: meaning "of the same kind" which suggests that our home is an extension of ourselves. The word *inhabit* derives from the Latin *habere*, which originally meant "to hold" either in offering or receiving. To inhabit literally means to be held within a habit. Habit has an interior and an exterior meaning: habits are patterns of thought or behavior of which we are largely unconscious. A habit is also clothing worn on the body, the garments of a nun or monk. Both meanings of the word habit are embodied, one through a level of consciousness within, the other as the outwardly worn symbol of allegiance or state of mind. But the richness of this meaning, the action verb of dwelling and inhabiting has vanished. "Language withdraws . . . its simple and high speech," wrote Heidegger, "but its primal call does not thereby become incapable of speech; it merely falls silent."[8]

In *The Poetics of Space* Gaston Bachelard suggested that if we were to search among the wealth of our vocabulary for verbs that express the dynamics of shelter and refuge, "we should find images based on animal movements . . . movements that are engraved in our muscles."[9] For Victor Hugo's Quasimodo, Notre Dame was successively, "egg, nest, house, country, universe." Hugo cautioned that, "It is useless to warn the reader not to take literally the figures of speech that I am obliged to use here to express the strange, symmetrical, immediate, almost consubstantial flexibility of a man and his edifice."[10] Our habitat protects our vulnerability, shelters, feeds, and sustains our dreams. This need, engraved as it is in our circuitry, is the deeper dimension of dwelling. Truly housing ourselves both expresses and responds to this longing for nest and shell. "*Only if we are capable of dwelling, only then can we build,*" wrote Heidegger.

The natural world teems with examples of the "consubstantial flexibility" of organism and artifice. In his marvelous book, *L'Oiseau,* Jules Michelet poetically writes, "A bird is a worker without tools. It has neither the hand of the squirrel, nor the teeth of the beaver . . . A bird's tool is its own body, that is its breast, with which he presses and tightens its materials until they have become absolutely pliant, well blended and adapted to the general plan." The bird makes a home with her body, for her body, whose form is "commanded from the inside". The size of the curve of her nest is determined precisely from the diameter of her body. The bird is truly building from the inside out, using her body as the tool to give shape to her home. "The house is a bird's very person; it is its form and most immediate effort, I shall even say, its suffering. The result is only obtained by constantly repeated pressure of the breast. There is not one of these blades of grass that, in order to make it curve and hold the curve, has not been pressed on countless times by the bird's breast, its heart."[12]

Michelet muses, "It would be interesting to find out if the forms birds give their nests, without ever having seen a nest, have not some analogy to their own inner constitutions."[13] This penetrating insight uncovers the key to what is so sorely lacking in our own built habitat. Our buildings do not suit us because they are tailored to fit an infinitesimal portion of our humanity. They are designed, as the Finnish architect Juhani Pallasmaa so eloquently says, to house "the intellect and the eye but . . . [leave] the body and the other senses, as well as our memories, imagination and dreams, homeless."[14] In their seminal book, *Body, Memory, and Architecture*, Kent Bloomer and Charles Moore conclude, "What is missing from our dwellings today are the potential transactions between body, imagination, and environment."[15]

When we design and build the tangible world we support certain features of our experience while suppressing others. Just as elements in the fabric of spoken language express a cosmology, the language of architecture manifests the value system that created it. "We make the obvious world by building it, and in constructing the world, we build ourselves, including the structure of our consciousness," writes E.V. Walter. "The way in which people habitually and consciously combine or orchestrate three worlds of the mind—the domain of common sense, the intellect, the imagination—gives form to their structure of consciousness."[16] Archaic people, for example, lived in a world dominated by the mythopoetic imagination in contrast to our modern framework of consciousness which is governed by the intellect. Yet our reluctance to reinforce the mythic imagination does not mean that modernity has extinguished myths. Mythical thinking remains alive and well, but its expression has migrated to another place. Analogous to Heidegger's interpretation of language, because our buildings have fallen silent, the primal voice they once fulfilled has sought satisfaction elsewhere.

As designers of the obvious world, we must not miss the opportunity to design for enduring human needs. Architecture, through means unique to it, can shelter our larger body and offer a perch on which the imagination can roost. Our built environment can cradle our unconscious desires rather than exploit them. Technology has taken over mental functions that were once filled in a tangible way. While not disparaging the marvels and importance of our advanced technology, we need to recognize its inability to satisfy certain perennial human needs. Ultimately neither technological means nor commodified products are capable of responding to the complex longings of the human heart.

A growing number of architects and thinkers have come to similar conclusions and offer their guidance. Pallasmaa wisely argues for an architecture that "seeks to accommodate rather than impress, evoke domesticity and comfort, rather than admiration and awe."[17] Bachelard recommends that "If we were to work at our dwelling-places the way Michelet dreams of his nest, we should not be wearing ready-made clothes . . . On the contrary, each one of us would have a personal house of his own, a nest for his body, padded to his measure."[18] The bird and her nest offer a potent metaphor, and like all rich metaphors its multilayered meaning unravels through time. Instinctively creating her nest, the bird uses her own body and specifically her heart. For her, "Everything is a matter of inner pressure, physically dominant intimacy. The nest is the swelling fruit pressing against its limits."[19] It is the boundary created from her own interior. Atop a stair landing in the pavilion at Taliesin West, Frank Lloyd Wright etched the words of Lao Tzu: "The reality of a building is the space inside to be lived in." He created buildings from the inside out. The bird starts from her own nerves and tissues.[20]

The pioneering psychologist J.J. Gibson coined many concepts that are now in mainstream usage. In *The Ecological Approach to Visual Perception* he showed that perception in animals, including humans, could not be understood without reference to the environment in which the animal lives. No hard demarcation exists between the observer and the environment; they are interdependent and complementary. The interaction between the organism and the environment could be understood in terms of natural units, which he called nested units. While his description may seem straightforward enough, it refutes the timeworn tradition of applying absolute metric units of space and time to living phenomena. Proportions when nested are relative to the size of the organism and radiate from the inside outward. Appropriate form and proportion of animal and environment are reciprocal to one another. Gibson writes,

> Boulders and soil are nested within canyons, which are in turn nested within mountains. This nesting is not hierarchical, but involves interesting overlaps. Thus, there is no preferred metric, no one scale of fundamental units, in terms of which the environment can be described . . . The unit you choose for describing the environment depends on the level of the environment you choose to describe . . . In particular, then, there is no privilege or fundamental description of the environment possible in terms of elementary particles or in terms of chemical structure . . . The framework for physical events is different from the framework of ecological events . . . We cannot describe the latter purely in terms of the former.[21]

Infected by the same disease that has plagued the social and biological sciences, architectural practice adopted the theoretical framework of physics and engineering. Impressed by the rapid success of the physical sciences after Newton, Enlightenment philosophers figured that the social sciences and planning would follow a similar course. Yet this approach has actually impaired the healthy development of the living sciences and ultimately contributed to the wholesale sense that individuals are replacement parts in a machine, strictly regulated and dispensable. "In transcending the metaphor of the world as a machine," writes Fritof Capra, "we also have to abandon the view that physics is the basis of all science . . . Different but mutually consistent concepts may be used to describe different aspects and levels of reality, without the need to reduce the phenomena of any level to those of the other."[22]

Gibson's nested units offer a pattern for understanding the irreducible dynamic interplay of human habitation. Nesting embodies the manner in which living systems are networks within networks whose information propagates through countless intricately woven nonlinear pathways. The French phenomenologist Merleau-Ponty describes nesting when he writes, "Each of the levels in which we successively live makes its appearance when we cast anchor in some setting which is offered to us. This setting itself is spatially particularized only for the previously given level."[23] The natural world consists, according to Capra, of "multileveled structures of systems within systems. Each of these forms a whole with respect to its parts while the same time being part of a larger whole. Thus cells combine to form tissues, tissues to form organs, and organs to form organisms. These in turn exist within social systems and ecosystems. Throughout the living world we find living systems nesting within other living systems."[24]

We are nested in a material embrace. Our mind is nested inextricably within our body as we are nested in the felt curve of home; home is nested successively in landscape, city, and world. Dwelling is not passive but positive, an action verb. Our nests are our mirrors, we can only make what is inside of us. Coleridge wrote, "For all we see, hear, feel and touch, the substance is and must be in ourselves ... all things shall live in us and we shall live in all things that surround us."[25]

Advances in the cognitive sciences have radically expanded our understanding of our relationship with the world we inhabit. Considering the implications of these recent findings in the context of our built habitat is the adventure of this book. Seeing, feeling, touching, listening to, and tasting such a spectrum is necessarily interdisciplinary. Sensory modalities and modes of knowing that we typically compartmentalize, must loosen and overlap. This is an open-ended exploration of potential interactions and hidden voices that live within our built world, not a compendium of agreed upon facts codified into conventional categories.

"I am not so much interested in ethics or morals," wrote the founder of deep ecology, Arne Naess. "I am interested in how we experience the world."[26] Our experience of the world is a fusion between the internal landscape of our minds and our constructed reality. In this "mental ecology," to use Pallasmaa's term, our body is the pivotal point of interface. Grounded and bounded in our flesh, finding ease in our harness may be our saving grace.

Herning Center for Art, Steven Holl

2

THE MIND OF THE SKIN

A poetry impure as the clothing we wear, or our bodies, soup stained,
soiled with our shameful behavior, our wrinkles and vigils
and dreams, observations and prophecies, declarations of loathing
and love, idylls and beasts, the shock of encounter, political loyalties,
denials and doubts, affirmations and taxes.

The holy canons of madrigal, the mandates of touch, smell, taste, sight,
hearing, the passion for justice, sexual desire, the sea sounding—
willfully rejecting and accepting nothing; the deep penetration of
things in the transports of love, a consummate poetry soiled by
the pigeon's claw, ice-marked and tooth marked, bitten delicately
with our sweat drops and usage perhaps. Till the instrument played
without respite yield us its solacing surfaces, and the wood show the
thorniest suavities shaped by the pride of the tool. Blossom and water
and wheat kernel share one precious consistency,
the sumptuous appeal of the tactile.

– Pablo Neruda

Freshly born or creased with time, our skin is our original medium of communication, our most primary contact with the world. An exquisitely selective, permeable boundary, skin is both envelope and organ. When we shiver, our skin betrays our ancient origin; the swollen pores of our goose bumps once held feathers. Our skin bears our signature; in a galaxy of innumerable possibilities, the spiral of our fingerprint is unique. Ebony, bone, or clay, our skin's tone traces the geography of our ancestors, was colored by the minerals and angle of the sun on their land. Our skin wraps us outside and in. In love's expression, the inside of our skin greets that of another. Snakes aren't the only ones who shed their flesh; every minute we cast off tens of thousands of skin cells. Skin is our most adaptive tissue. By the time we turn fifty, we have worn out and replaced over 600 skins, each one a slightly different reflection of our habits, growth, and overall health. Our skin translucently reveals our emotional states, both our rose blush and our blanched pallor mirror events that occur deep in the viscera. Our skin regulates our metabolism and is directly controlled by autonomic neural signals in the brain and chemical signals from myriad sources. People die from severe burns not because they have lost an essential part of their sense of touch. They die because they have lost an indispensable organ.

Ashley Montagu opens his beautiful book, *Touching*, with a chapter entitled "The Mind of the Skin". In it he describes the skin, "the mother of the senses," as the visible surface of a continuously interconnected system whose molecules are linked together in an intricate web work. The human body is indeed the sum of thousands of physiological processes functioning in concert with one another in an integrated matrix that has no fundamental unit, no central aspect, and no part that is more primary or basic than any other. An effect on one part of the body cascades through all of the other parts; the properties of the whole depend on the integrated activities of each. "We touch heaven when we lay our hands on a human body," wrote Novalis.[1]

The mind of the skin captures what cognitive scientists and philosophers mean when they speak about embodiment. The mind is not centralized in the brain, it is intricately manifested in the integrated whole of our viscera and tissue and extends beyond the surface of our skin in interaction and participation with our environment. The mind is in our breath and heartbeat, each a culmination of countless mechanical, vibrational, oscillatory, energetic, and informational events. Merleau-Ponty was developing his notion of the "flesh" before he died suddenly in an automobile accident in Paris. The description of the flesh in his unfinished manuscript, *The Visible and the Invisible*, is astonishingly similar to the embodied mind. Neither "subject nor object, but their connective tissue," it is a sensing and sensible material latticework.[2] Similarly, skin is the tentacle of a sensing subject, both filter and extension of our nervous system.

Though the skin is our efficient protector, it bruises and is easily cut. The concept of the flesh, the mind of the skin, overturns the millennial assumption that forms a cornerstone of Western thought. For centuries, we've been told that our souls are imprisoned in this carnal form, that our body is not the path to heaven that Novalis suggested, but an impediment to be endured. Our science, philosophy, and religion have taught, as William Blake wrote, "that man has two real existing principles, a body and a soul; that energy alone is from the body, while reason alone is from the soul; and that God will torment men eternally for following his energies."[3]

The decisive cleavage of the mind from the body occurred during the Copernican Revolution, a period whose scientific achievements are rivalled only by our own. Seeds that had lain dormant in the soil of previous ages reached fruition during this period because advances in mathematics, mechanics, anatomy, and astronomy that had paralleled one another, finally coalesced. As Lewis Mumford has pointed out, there was not a single idea in the new scientific world picture that had not existed in some form before.[4] The Copernican worldview was the result of a uniquely human intellect, while at the same time excluding the rest of human experience. The invention of the telescope enabled Galileo to cast his eye not upon earth, but heavenward. At once the sun commanded the orbiting planets and dispelled the flimsy shadows in Plato's cave to reveal the absolute perfection of Platonic form.

> On this new assumption the cosmos itself was primarily a mechanical system capable of being fully understood by reference solely to a mechanical model. Not man, but the machine became the central feature in this new world picture: hence the chief end of human existence was to confirm this system by utilizing and controlling the energies derived from the sun, reshaping every part of the environment in conformity to the Sun God's strict commands. In the acceptance of the mechanical orthodoxy man was to find his salvation.[5]

Lewis Mumford wrote this passage in 1964. His assessment may be of mythic proportion, but if you find it extreme, consider the size and quantity of cars and buildings fueled by ancient sunlight, the unquestioning mass consumption of plastic and petroleum products, the average person's mountain of debt despite a forty hour work week, and the steady escalation of earth's basal temperature.

Centuries of the human yearning for transcendence were funneled through the lens of the telescope. The thrilling vision of perfect spheres orbiting the sun in mathematically predictable trajectories, isolated from one another, unburdened of embarrassing human entanglements, defined the new world picture. Abstraction seized the Western mind; the new world of light and space, order and beauty offered a refuge from the savagery and superstition that was commonplace in the sixteenth century. The earth rotated cleanly, the pendulum swung with the accurate motion of a clock. Not only earth, but the heavens could be mapped and determined, and territories could be carved up with chilling disregard for any value that did not conform to the dictates of the machine.

We are fashioned indelibly by our tools: the unprecedented augmentation of the eye permitted what was once only imagined to be actually witnessed. The modern technologic and scientific transformation to which we are heirs is rooted in a world picture that was shaped by the tools of the seventeenth century and the ideological framework articulated by René Descartes. His *Discourse on Method* synthesized mathematical and mechanical reasoning and equipped men to be "the lords and possessors of nature." In that statement he perhaps unwittingly voiced the unspoken sociopolitical motives of his century. His allegiance to the absolutism of both the church and baroque patriarchy consolidated the strength of his enterprise.

Mumford has shown that Cartesian solopcism was a natural outgrowth of baroque absolutism. Descartes praised the princely ability to act alone in the spotlight of center stage toward a single end. His process of cleansing the mind of all knowledge in order to start clean with *tabula rasa* can be likened to the "stripping away of constituent groups that compose any real community—the family, the village, the farm, the church, the guild . . . in trying to make a fresh start, Descartes had in fact swept away nothing. For without his collectively stored and individually remembered experience, Descartes' lips and tongue and vocal chords could not have framed his triumphant sentence, 'I think, therefore I am.'"[6] Severed from the living matrix, disembodied intelligence was all that remained of humanity. "The body of man," proclaimed Descartes, "*is nothing but* a statue or machine made of earth."[7]

While modern science recognizes the limits of the mechanical worldview engineered by Galileo, Descartes, and Newton it continues to bear their imprimatur and remains as Schrodinger observed, devoid of "blue, yellow, bitter, sweet, beauty, delight, sorrow."[8] Scientific inquiry has not yet fully recovered from humanity's exile. Divorcing the body from the mind offered a tidy solution to the intractable complexity of the human experience. The simplicity is so tempting that we need not to venture far to hear its refrain: scientists hotly pursue the single *mechanism* that will expose the mystery in their respective fields. The attitude looms behind every characterization of the mind as a software program and the apotheosis of technology as ultimate savior.

As untenable as it now seems, the disincarnate mind reigned virtually unchallenged until the late nineteenth century when, as Alfred North Whitehead pointed out, the science of physiology reinstalled the mind back into nature.[9] The study of the body turned out to be a historic hinge. The theory of natural selection served to make the already problematic mind/body separation more acute, but most philosophers simply ignored Darwin's theory, preferring the safety of the well-primed path of a priori speculation. But less than a century later, a new body of scientific knowledge emerged that was so important, even philosophers were forced to pay attention. This knowledge developed within the biological disciplines that study the evolution, structure, and processes of the nervous system, whose primary mission is to understand the functioning of cognition and the human brain. Scientific methodology, as framed by Galileo et al., has proved to be insufficient in this enterprise.

Copernican in magnitude, the paradigm shift precipitated by the cognitive sciences shifts our attention intensely toward the earth and our own minds. This new understanding of the world situates our humanity in a cosmos that is not sterile or isolated, but intricately patterned, brilliantly interrelated, and teeming with life. As the neuroscientist Antonio Damasio puts it, "A comprehensive understanding of the human mind requires an organismic perspective; that not only must the mind move from the nonphysical *cogitum* to the realm of biological tissue, but it also must be related to the whole organism possessed of an integrated body proper and brain and fully interactive with a physical and social environment."[10] The body and mind are not only inextricably linked; they are functionally interdependent with the environment. The work of the cognitive scientists can potentially heal the rupture between reason and emotion, philosophy, science, and everyday life. The neuroscientist Candace Pert writes, "We can no longer think of the emotions as having less validity than the physical, material substance, but instead, see them as cellular signals that are involved in the process of translating information into physical reality, literally transforming mind into matter. Emotions are at the nexus between matter and mind, going back between the two and influencing both."[11]

Architecture, material in its very nature, literally touches us daily. It is a discipline that bridges technics and art, the individual and his or her environment. The separation between the mind and the body that dislocated the intellect from emotion and philosophy from daily life has had deleterious consequences for the built environment. The reinsertion of the mind/body into the very nexus of our thought offers an urgent opportunity. The esteemed architectural historian Sigfried Giedion wrote:

> Social, economic and functional influences play a vital part in all human activities, from the sciences to the arts. But there are other factors which have to be taken into account—our feelings

and emotions. These factors are often dismissed as trivial, but actually their effect upon men's actions is immense. A good share of the misfortunes of the past century came out of its belief that industry and techniques had only a functional import, with no emotional content. The arts were exiled to an isolated realm of their own, completely isolated from everyday realities. As a result, life lost unity and balance; science and industry made steady advances, but in the now detached realm of feeling there was nothing but a vacillation from one extreme to the other.[12]

The exclusive reliance on the intellect and the valuation of reason as the supreme human faculty is largely responsible for the creation of buildings that exhibit contempt for humanity rather than providing an invitation to dwell. One cannot help but compare the flat landscape of modernist buildings to Galileo's view through the telescope: isolated formal objects bereft of the human presence, "fit for machines to live in."[13] The new world of light and space authored by Galileo and Newton found its impress in Le Corbusier's *New World of Space*, in which he describes a natural setting of flowers, trees and mountains to "command attention because of their independent forms. It is because they are seen to be isolated from their context."[14] The glorification of the isolated object in denial of context is so entrenched that Kenneth Frampton has called ours a species that "can think of nothing better to do than to go on proliferating freestanding objects."[15]

Juhani Pallasmaa's prescient critique of ocularcentrism uncovers part of the problem. "The privileging of the sense of sight over the other senses is an inarguable theme in Western thought, and it is also an evident bias in the architecture of our century . . . The problems arise from the isolation of the eye outside its natural interaction with other sense modalities, and from the elimination and suppression of other senses, which increasingly reduce and restrict the experience of the world into the sphere of vision."[16] Ocularcentrism is symptomatic of a deeper fallacy: we are more than our eyes, more than our intellect. The design of our circuitry and evolution of our bodies, as we develop from infancy to adulthood, is shaped by our activities and the manner in which our bio-circuitry integrates our interactions with the world. We can no longer conceive of our brain and behavior within the constricted categories of nature versus nurture or genes versus experience. "Neither our brains nor our minds are tabula rasa when we are born. Neither are they fully determined genetically," writes Damasio.[17]

Environmental circumstances promote or retard the healthy functioning of an organism. An impoverished built environment fosters human atrophy. The cultural anthropologist Edward T. Hall pointed out over fifty years ago that, "The relationship between *man and the cultural dimension is one in which man and his environment participate in molding each other.*"[18] Our immediate evolution has shifted from our body to our extensions. We suffer grave consequences if we fail to heed these well-supported insights. The cognitive philosopher Andy Clark similarly warns that,

> We must begin to face up to some rather puzzling (dare I say metaphysical?) questions. For starters, the nature and bounds of the intelligent agent look increasingly fuzzy. Gone is the central executive of the brain—the real boss who organizes and integrates all activities of multiple special-purpose subsystems. And gone is the neat boundary between the thinker (the bodiless intellectual engine) and the thinker's world. In place of this comforting image . . . it may for some purposes be wise to consider the intelligent system as a spatio-temporally extended process not limited to the tenuous envelope of skin and skull . . . the flow of reasons and thoughts, and the temporal evolution of ideas and attitudes, are

determined and explained by the intimate, complex, continued interplay of brain, body and world.[19]

We would do well to begin from the ecology of the skin in its organismic complexity. Few substances in our world possess the plasticity, protection, and filtering porosity of the skin, which is both marvelous and familiar. Understanding his buildings as extended bodies, Peter Zumthor writes,

> Here we are sitting in this barn, there are these rows of beams and they are in turn covered . . . that is what I would call the first and greatest secret of architecture, that it collects different things in the world, different materials, and combines them to create a space like this. To me it's a kind of anatomy we're talking about. Really, I mean the word 'body' quite literally. It's like our own bodies with their anatomy and things we can't see and skin covering us—that is what architecture means to me and that is how I try to think about it. As a bodily mass, a membrane, a fabric, a kind of covering cloth, velvet, silk, all around me. The body! Not the idea of the body—the body itself! A body that can touch me.[20]

The boundary that divides us from the world is not at all clean-cut, as Andy Clark points out. This shift in understanding expands our notion of what a building is and what it can be and do. What if we consider our buildings as membranes that cover us and so design for the body itself, creating buildings that, like skin, are themselves a medium of communication and primary ground of contact, places that hold us in their creases and folds.

We are both fragile and invincible, we are cut and we heal. Our architecture, if it is to be poetic, must shelter this vulnerability.

In the dignified company of Neruda, our architecture can be an impure poetry:

> Let no one forget them: despondent, old mawkishness impure and flawed fruits of a fabulous species lost to the memory, cast away in a frenzy's abandonment—moonlight, the swan in the gathering darkness, all the hackneyed endearments: surely that is the poet's occasion, essential and absolute.

> Those who shun the 'bad taste' of things will fall on their face in the snow.[21]

3

ADIEU, DESCARTES

If your ears see
And eyes hear,
Not a doubt you'll cherish—
How naturally the rain drips
From the eaves!

– Bujutsu Sasho

"I shall now close my eyes, I shall stop my ears, I shall call away all of my senses," proclaimed Descartes, who dutifully followed a long line of predecessors in mistrusting his senses. Sensory information contaminated the pure certainty of his mind, the locus of reason. Since Plato, reason was considered to be the supreme faculty distinguishing man from beast. Vision, the soldier of reason, was considered the most trustworthy instrument of the conscious mind. When Aristotle itemized the senses into five discrete, hierarchical categories, vision topped the list. The fruit of reason was philosophy, which according to Plato was the greatest good that "ever was or will be given by the gods to mortal men." Without sight, philosophy would not be possible, "for had we never seen the stars and the sun and heaven, none of the words which we have spoken about the universe would ever have been uttered." Behind the esteemed position of sight trailed hearing, followed by smell and taste, while touch ranked last. Not coincidentally, the hierarchy of the senses was mirrored in the social order of Plato's ideal Republic: philosophers were guardians who were served by warriors, leaving artisans and farmers just above slaves.[1]

But fissures are forming in the exclusive dominion of the eye. The tools we have developed to augment vision, the electron microscope and the Hubble telescope, have stretched our views into macro and micro scales previously unimaginable. The advent of magnetic resonance imaging has opened entirely new possibilities for our understanding of the mind. Our vision has expanded to such an extent, that it is no longer tenable to consider the eyes in isolation from or privileged over our other sensory faculties. William Blake's appraisal of the senses as the "chief inlets of the soul," is a more accurate understanding of the senses.

Though sight is inarguably important, the senses cannot be compartmentalized. The senses function in unison, almost inseparably from one another and it is "through our senses we know substantially all that we know," confirms Louis Sullivan. He said, "The imagination, intuition, reason are all but exalted forms of the physical senses. For man there is nothing but the physical for what he calls spirituality is but the most exalted reach of his animalism."[2] We are finally awakening to our long neglected senses. "This growing awareness represents something of an overdue insurgency against the painful deprivation of sensory experience we have suffered in our technologized world," writes Ashley Montagu.[3]

An abundance of scientific theories compete to explain how sense perception actually works. J.J. Gibson rejected the conventional notion of the senses as passive receptors that respond to their respective forms of mechanical, optical, or chemical energy. Instead, he considered the senses as active perceptual organs which function as systems. Perceptual systems coordinate complex multi-dimensional environmental information that refuses quantification. The brain does not reconstruct a cluster of sensations or process information like a computer. To understand perception, Gibson compared the senses to tentacles or feelers that extract environmental information from a kaleidoscopic array of ambient energy. We gain information about the world through actively resonating with our environment. When modeled as active perceptual systems, our senses can be classified as five modes of external attention. Gibson identified these modes of attention as the basic orienting system, the auditory system, the haptic system, the tasting and smelling system, and the visual system.[4] Perception occurs through sensory modalities braided together inextricably like the roots of trees in a thick forest.

Because the senses are not mere channels of signals and sensations, perceptual abilities can be refined with practice and attention. When perception is understood as active externally-oriented attention, the relationship between the animal and the environment becomes paramount. According to Gibson, an animal does not so much live in its environment, as the environment is an extension of the animal.[5] The two coexist in a mutually interdependent, constantly evolving relationship. Charles Darwin describes this interactive alliance in one of his more poetic passages of *On the Origin of Species*, where he observes that a flower fertilized by the wind is destitute of both color and nectar, while those frequented by insects are honey rich, brilliantly colored and bear open petals of invitation. This led him to conclude that, "If insects had not developed on the face of the earth, our plants would not be decked with beautiful flowers."[6] Accordingly, birds disseminate the seeds of luscious red berries and female animals of all sorts prefer their males to be gorgeously patterned. "We may infer from all of this that a nearly similar taste for beautiful colors and for musical sounds runs through a large part of the animal kingdom . . . how the sense of beauty in its simplest form—that is, the reception of a peculiar kind of pleasure from certain colors, forms, and sounds—was first developed in the mind of man . . . is a very obscure subject."[7]

That obscure subject is the study of aesthetics, the translation of the Greek word *aesthetikos*, which means sense-perception. Aesthetic pleasure, the longing for beauty, according to Darwin, is an evolutionary impulse. Gibson used the term affordance to characterize the attractive force with which beauty binds us to our environment. An affordance describes the possibilities for action that are latent in the environment and expresses the complementarity between animal and environ. Gibson said, "The possibilities of the environment and the way of life of the animal go together almost inseparably."[8] Product designers have appropriated the notion of an affordance to encourage intuitive usability. If the potential capabilities latent in a product are highlighted with color or seductive form, the product is easier and more enjoyable to use. Think of an iPhone: it fits neatly into your palm; the text rotates, shrinks or grows according to your slightest touch. Responsive, attractive, easy to use, it is a tool that anticipates your needs through suggesting its own dormant possibilities.

Innate desire enables us to identify opportunities within the environment that will satisfy our needs and purposes. Natural changes such as ripening, flowering, and decay, for example, signify a change in affordance, these events then catalyze corresponding shifts in an animal's plumage, hair, or skin. An affordance illustrates the manner in which information about the self is provoked by and coincides with information about the environment. "They are inseparable. Ego-reception accompanies extero-reception, like the other side of a coin," writes Gibson.[9] Feedback from the environment shapes our perception in a subjective and objective polarity; one perceives the environment and co-perceives oneself within that environment. You can almost hear Merleau-Ponty's voice when he said we are "an open circuit to be completed by the earth and vice versa."[10]

Gibson complained when his fellow psychologists climbed on the computer bandwagon in the 1960s. He adamantly refused to allow them to preempt the term information without re-examining the notion that perception is the processing of input. Information about living systems is not to be understood in a computational or literary sense. Gibson used information in its verb sense, as it derives from the Latin *informare*, meaning to bring into form. Like Darwin's observation of the aesthetic proclivities of birds and bees, perception is an event of resonance between the individual and her environment, not an indirect, intellectualized model of reality.

Our experience of color wonderfully illustrates our reciprocal relationship with the environment. "Color is where the brain and the universe meet," observed Merleau-Ponty.[11] When we look at the sky, the color blue that we see is not a property existing independently in the sky. The experience of color is a dynamic interplay between the wavelengths in the electromagnetic spectrum reflected by objects, ambient lighting conditions, the various color cones in our retinas that absorb the corresponding wavelengths, and the complex neural circuitry connected to these cones. An apple is red because it absorbs the longer wavelengths of the light spectrum and reflects the red wavelengths. Merleau-Ponty called red "a certain woof of the simultaneous and successive."[12] The great psychologist William James said that, "The nervous system of every living thing is but a bundle of predispositions to react in particular ways upon the contact of particular features of the environment."[13] Analogous to our experience of color, our personal network of predispositions combine in a complex interplay with environmental factors. We reflect shorter or longer wavelengths, as it were, which tint and filter our life experiences.

The experience of listening, looking, feeling, and tasting results from our unique polyphony of personal, biological, environmental, social, and cultural factors, in a dynamic interplay that is neither entirely subjective nor wholly objective. Examining the role of cultural codes in determining our habits of perception is the subject of the book, *The Varieties of Sensory Experience*. In this work, the authors convincingly demonstrate that the sensory order is inextricably bound together with the cultural order.[14] The extent to which various cultures value and thus channel and reinforce certain sensory orders produces differences in their ways of knowing.[15] The practitioners of Siddhi medicine in India, for instance, are rigorously trained to hear six different pulses where we only hear one. The synaesthetic Incan people of the Andes prize the image of the rainbow because it possesses the power to evoke all of the senses. Their language reflects this valuation: a single word describes "the concentrated sweetness of dried fruit and also pleasant speech and a soft tactile sensation."[16] This word also refers to the rainbow effect common in their weaving.

For the Hausa people of northern Nigeria, the verb *ji* designates the summation of all of the non-visual senses. *Ji* not only refers to hearing, tasting, smelling, and touching, it also means 'to feel' in an emotional sense and to 'know' in a cognitive sense. The verb that means 'to see' is rarely used in common parlance. Isolating thinking from feeling is alien to the Hausa. Their fusion of the sense faculties precludes privileging one sense over another, yet one can detect a gustatory bias in their proverbs. Two of their aphorisms are, "seeing is not eating" and "a man is like pepper, until you chew him you do not know how hot he can be."[17] Tasting is an accurate gauge used to test the inner character of a person or a thing. Knowing is not abstract, it is physically internalized through one's mouth, is metabolized and integrated into one's tissues and bones.

Just as words within the fabric of spoken language reflect a cosmology, so too does the language of architecture embody the value system that created it. Features within the physique of the built-environment support or suppress our innate predispositions and thus frame our experience of the world. Considering the built environment aesthetically, that is from the perspective of our various perceptual systems, helps identify opportunities to appeal to more than reason and to elicit a more complex interaction between our bodies, our imagination, and our environment.

The 'basic orienting system' is the frame of reference for all of the other perceptual systems. Gravity is its principal orienting force. This system comprises the vestibular organs in our inner ear that function in harmony with our eyes and our proprioceptive sense of weight to organize our experience into basic vertical and horizontal planes. The ecologist Paul Shepard suggested that, "Perhaps our aesthetic feeling for symmetry and balance, our inclination to abstract the vertical and horizontal lines and follow them with our eyes, belongs to the following of trunks and limbs, first with bodies, then by sitting and looking."[18] The weight of built masses and materials evokes deep comfort because they recall this primary pull. The very proportion of our body and bones reflects our intrinsic tie to the gravitational tug of our planet. Maybe it is alignment with this fundamental force to which Zen Master Yagyu Tajima alludes when he counsels, "See first with the mind, then with the eyes, and finally with the torso and limbs."[19] Indeed, through techniques that still the mind and refine the senses, martial artists become sensitive to quiet energetic murmurs that most of us miss; some can even detect magnetic north when blindfolded.[20]

Our vestibular system orients us to the earth's gravitational field and functionally overlaps our auditory system. The cochlear organs in the middle ear and auricle that comprise our auditory system are designed so remarkably its evolution has remained unchanged from fish to man.[21] This system orients us to sound and airborne vibrations. In Gibson words, it is "designed for listening, hearing is incidental."[22] Like our experience of color, sound is also a relational pattern, a configuration, and not a set of absolute frequencies. The only naturally occurring sounds are tone spectrums, not isolated tones.[23] Natural sounds appear as undulating waves when graphed on paper, each wave slightly different from the next. It was not until the Industrial Revolution that the flat line was introduced into the soundscape.[24] Prolonged sounds that remain unchanged over the course of night and day can only be produced artificially. Highly redundant, anemic of information, the flat line in sound is rarely found in nature.[25] Since sound and architecture are profoundly related, this absence of rhythm is not without consequence.

Long before Goethe called architecture 'frozen music' the two art forms had been compared to one another. Both are immersive; music surrounds us, just as architecture does. We are inside of a building in the same way that we are surrounded in music. And unlike the eyes, we cannot close our ears, which explains why we feel more vulnerable to sound. The first sound that anyone has ever heard is the pulse of the mother's heartbeat. Our earliest unconscious memory is the rhythmic bath we experienced inside our mother's body. That is perhaps why, prior to the invention of the metronome, the tempo of music was based on the human pulse. The capacity to synchronize with surrounding rhythms is innate; an infant begins

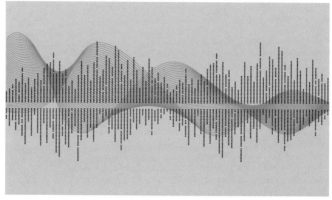

Sonograph reading of jazz music

to hear in the womb and immediately following birth the infant entrains rhythmically with her mother's voice. After birth, a mother tends to hold her newborn upon her left breast, over her heart, regardless of whether she is right or left handed.[26]

If our spatial relation concepts are shaped by our bodily experience, as the cognitive scientists tell us, we could infer that rhythmic synchronization is intimately linked with subsequent spatial experience. The underlying pattern shaped by myriad collective activities and rituals, bodily sensations and history that conspire to create culture could be called that culture's rhythm. In fact, E.T. Hall calls music "the rhythmic consensus of the culture."[27] In *Experiencing Architecture*, Steen Eiler Rasmussen writes, "There is something mysterious about the stimulating effect of rhythm. You can explain what it is that creates rhythm but you have to experience it yourself to know what it is like. A person listening to music experiences rhythm as something beyond all reflection, as something existing within himself. A man who moves rhythmically starts the motion himself and feels that he controls it. But very shortly the rhythm controls him; he is possessed by it, it carries him along."[28] Sensing rhythm is exhilarating because it occurs without conscious effort. We have all experienced a dance or music performance or an athletic event, in which the players on stage or in the field are moving in a rhythm so palpable that it becomes contagious. Like a flock of birds synchronized in flight, we become swept up and absorbed in the rhythm. Such an experience recalls Zeno's paradox: "If a bushel of corn turned out upon the floor makes a noise, each grain and each part of each grain must make a noise likewise, but, in fact, this is not so."[29] Rhythm coordinates the sum of its parts to become something else. In rhythm the aggregation of parts is transformed into a unique whole quite unlike any one of the individual parts. This mystery is an ordinary fact of life, we are immersed in rhythms all of the time, but are generally unaware of them.

Rhythm is an underlying social, cultural, and environmental pattern and we can, as architects, compose symphonies. But we rarely seize

upon opportunities for resonance. Frank Lloyd Wright said that when he saw architecture that moved him he heard music in his inner ear.[30] We are certainly not all synaesthetes; instead our situation is closer to the composer Murray Shafer's assessment that "the modern architect is designing for the deaf."[31] From an acoustic perspective, dwelling in most buildings is equivalent to being locked in an elevator doomed to listen to muzak. To further stretch the analogy, his words have unfortunately fallen on deaf ears, while vast acoustic opportunities lie dormant in surface form, texture, and contour. "All knowledge rests on sensitivity," Gibson reminds us.[32] The vast majority of our buildings are designed by the eye for the eye, and in the process, our ears have become desensitized.

To tune in to this rich, invisible world, we can learn volumes from the blind whose landscape is a field of reverberation and echo. They navigate using echolocation, the perception of echoes. Echoes are reflections of sound whose waves alter according to the surfaces they encounter. The spatial sense of the blind is truly astonishing. Blind people can identify textures, sense the presence of small objects from two meters away and ride their bikes at impressive speeds through complex unfamiliar environments. One study identified a blind man who was able to reliably detect the presence of a one-inch disc from three feet away. [33]

An ability native to all of us, studies consistently show that sighted people can develop echolocation. Such findings prove that knowledge gained through listening can be cultivated and refined. Of course gifted musicians and composers have a natural advantage. When John Cage visited an anechoic chamber at Harvard he expected to hear silence, but instead he heard two sounds, one high and one low. "When I described them to the engineer in charge, he informed me that the high one was my nervous system in operation, the low one was my blood in circulation."[34] If you find that story amazing, imagine this: when eighteen different blind children were each isolated in an anechoic chamber, they were able to reliably detect a four by one foot wooden panel.[35] This means they not only heard the sound of their heartbeat and blood rushing through their veins, they also heard the echo of their internal symphony reverberating from the wooden panel! A world so subtle is indescribably different than the one we experience through our eyes.

The landscape of echo is one of mirrors and reflections. "Every reflection implies a doubling of sound by its ghost, hidden on the other side of the reflecting surface," muses Murray Shafer. "A far more potent image than Narcissus reflected in the water is that of Narcissus's alter-ego mocking his voice from unseen places behind the rocks."[36] Characterizing this multi-dimensional reverberant sound as energy underlies the Chinese practice of Feng Shui. Practitioners of the art consider an environment harmonious if it allows ambient energy, which they call *chi*, to circulate in an unencumbered yet balanced way. Through proper alignment of surfaces and objects, *chi* invigorates both interior and exterior spaces. Surface arrangement is not merely visual and is certainly not superficial at all. The shape, size, and relief in an interior space determine the tempo and pace of activities that can take place within it. This becomes particularly clear when studying the architectural forms of our ancient past.

Ancient cultures were strongly auditory. Oral traditions were the norm prior to the invention of the printing press, which solidified the hegemony of vision. The valuation and refinement of listening is critical to appreciating the extraordinary acoustic mastery of ancient civilizations. If you stand directly beneath the apex of the main cupola of the Shah Abbas Mosque in Isfahan, for example, you will hear your echo seven times. If you move as little as one foot

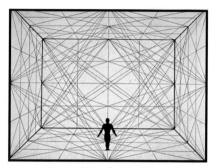

Figur und Raumlineatur, Oskar Schlemmer

to either side, you will hear nothing. "Experiencing this remarkable event one cannot help thinking that the echo was no mere by-product of visual symmetry but was intentionally engineered by designers who knew perfectly well what they were doing and perhaps even used the echo principle in determining the parabolic features of their cupolas," writes Shafer.[37]

The Mayans of ancient Mexico may have built their pyramids to function as immense musical instruments. According to archeologists, the temples were considered to be sacred mountains where clouds gathered and condensed rain. The sound of footsteps on the massive stairs that surround pyramids such as those at Chichen Itza sound curiously like echoing raindrops. Research suggests that the pyramids could have been built deliberately for the purpose of playing rain music. The pyramids are designed with varying configurations of stairs and landings, some are even while others are punctuated with platforms. When acoustic engineers compared the frequency of sounds produced by people walking up El Castillo, a hollow pyramid in the Yucatan with those generated at the solid,

Chichen Itza, Mexico

unevenly distributed staircase of the Moon Pyramid at Teotihua-can, in central Mexico, they discovered a striking similarity between the sound frequency at both sites. This suggests that the rain music resulted from the sound waves traveling through the steps and dif-fracting from the corrugated surfaces to produce the particular rain-drop sounding waves that propagate along the stairs.[38] Propitiation to the gods occurred through bodily participation with the medium of the temple. The temples were not strictly objects, but instruments played with the bodies of the supplicants. The music of skin on stone delivered the quenching rain.

The pressure of feet creating reverberant sound powerfully portrays an architecture that listens and touches. Touching is the mode of attention defined as the haptic system. Gibson developed the word *haptic*, from the Greek *haptikos*, which means pertaining to the sense of touch. Because of the tangible nature of buildings, the haptic sys-tem is perhaps the perceptual system par excellence for experienc-ing architecture. Information about the environment, literally being in touch with our world, comes through touch. Touching does not stop at the skin; it involves deformations of tissues, configuration of joints, and the stretching of muscle fibers through contact with the earth. In the haptic system, the hands and other body members are active organs of perception. In contemporary culture, the term haptic is most commonly used in the field of computer science and robot-ics. The next wave of computer design—haptics—explores ways in which hands and other body members can interface with computers.

Computer engineers are seizing opportunities to engage the per-ceptual organs of our haptic sense, but it is a non-priority for most architects. Perhaps we take the tactility of our work for granted. We fail to appreciate the opportunity and mandate to create work that truly engages our whole bodies. We are so mesmerized with the idea of space, we find it difficult to finally accept that absolute space was a notion invented for the sake of mathematical convenience. The space we actually do experience is the unique location of our body, our bones, and the angles of our joints. Each one of our joints is a sense organ that detects angles and gauges spatial relationships. Our joints are bound in tissues knit together in a matrix of liquid crystal. Liquid crystalline structures are the rule rather than the exception in natural systems. This connective tissue is the same gossamer steel that a spider excretes from her body to spin her web. This fabric of connective tissue is a semi-conducting information network. Within this latticework, each tension and compression generates bio-electric signals that precisely characterize our movements.

The touch receptors on the soles of your feet send messages to your brain every time you stand and put pressure on the ground. These messages combine in the brain with vestibular, visual, and other touch information to keep you on the 'tip of your toes'. Because these receptors blur with age, we tend to lose our balance as the years advance. In Europe, studies have shown that balance deteriorates more slowly in elderly people who walk regularly on cobblestones rather than on smooth modern sidewalks. The Chinese have long known this. In Taiwan "stone stepping" is a way of life for many people. Nearly every village has built special paths of pebble on which people walk barefoot for half an hour before they go to work. The foot massage afforded by the textured path has proven to increase health and wellness.

> Walking creates rhythmic compressions on bones and cartilage and cycles of tension in tendons. These processes lead to pulsating fields that spread through the body. Each impact of the foot on the surface leads to a veritable symphony of electromagnetic fields that tell a precise story of the force vectors developed with-

in the body fabric. Walking on grass will produce a totally different melody than walking on pavement. [39]

Paving in Prague

An architecture of touch responds to and modulates these subtly
cascading fields. "The mind includes more than the intellect. It
contains a history of what we learn through our feet," wrote E.V.
Walter.[40] Our designs are instruments that hold the potential to
play melodies or orchestrate symphonies. This means that we must
attend to the design of ramps, spirals, promenades, and pathways
that shape grand sweeping motions, with the same amount of careful consideration that goes into making the handle of a door. Both
dimensions of design touch us, their meaning is not exclusive to
their scale. Carlo Scarpa considered designing a chair more diffi-

cult than most architectural programs. Holding our torso and seat, supporting our spine, positioning our feet, and touching our skin, the chair is a universe onto itself. A chair can either offer a warm embrace or conduct heat away from our skin with scant regard for human comfort. Scarpa's sensitivity to detail was so accentuated that when asked to design a spoon he said that unless the spoon would establish a new relationship between its function and weight in the hand, any attempt to redesign it would be futile. After all, how many objects in our lives are we more intimate with than our spoon? It is this degree of intimacy, sensitivity, and humane vulnerability that is prerequisite for artful haptic design.

Born into Venice, Carlo Scarpa understood the fragile balance between tactility and evanescence. Barely a landmass, Venice knows the vulnerability of flux. Its buildings, partially submerged annually, are themselves bridges and at times seasonal boats. When commissioned to renovate the Fondazione Querini Stampalia, Scarpa allowed the surrounding water to flow inside the museum rather than damming the adjacent canal. Water is channeled through a bronze filigree screen around the perimeter and physically frames the rooms. One can move freely along Scarpa's catwalk-like platforms that have transformed formerly unusable rooms into sculptural encounters with the water that so defines Venice. Lushly detailed surfaces lead one to a garden, where water is again seduced from dripping pipes and guided through labyrinthine pools until it ushers into a lily pond. This garden is a multi-sensory feast: frequented by singing birds and filled with fragrant lilies and the sound of water in all of its motions.

Integrating gardens into our buildings is a time-honored way to invite aromas and flavors into our habitat. But the hermetically sealed character of many buildings neglects the olfactory character of a

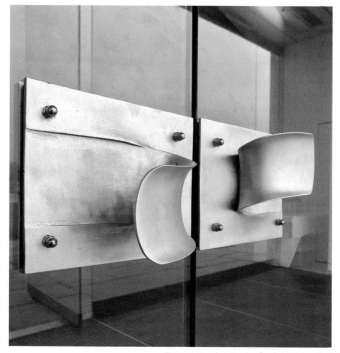

Door at Herning Center for Art, Steven Holl

place. E.T. Hall complained that, "The extensive use of deodorants and suppression of odor in public places results in a land of olfactory blandness and sameness that would be difficult to duplicate anywhere else in the world. This blandness makes for undifferentiated spaces and deprives us of richness and variety in life."[41] Our sense of smell is activated by the nature of volatile sources. *Vola*, means to fly; aromas then, must be allowed to freely fly through the air. Screens of skin-like porosity will naturally allure fragrance. A dwelling can inhale and exhale, protect and flow. One experiences such delicacy during a Japanese tea ceremony. Welcomed into an intricate garden, seated on tatami straw mats whose proportions derive directly from the human form, one is surrounded by paper walls whose fragility permits breathing in the atmosphere, while enhancing the sensation of the heat, sounds, and flavors that pivot about the iron pot of tea. In *Zen and Japanese Culture*, D.T. Suzuki describes such a teahouse, which has been designed and constructed according to a code passed down through generations.

> Where a series of flagstones irregularly arranged comes to a stop, there stands an insignificant-looking straw thatched hut, low and unpretentious to the last degree. The entrance is not by the door but by a sort of aperture; to enter through it, a visitor has to be shorn of all his encumbrances . . . The inside is a small semi-lighted room about ten feet square; the ceiling is low and of uneven height and structure. The posts are not smoothly planed and finished, they are mostly of natural wood. After a little while, however, the room grows gradually lighter as our eyes begin to adjust to the new situation. We notice an ancient looking *kake-momo* in the alcove . . . An incense burner emits a smoke of fragrance, which has the singular effect of soothing one's nerves. The flower vase does not contain more than a single flower stem, not at all gorgeous or ostentatious; but, like a little white lily blooming under a rock surrounded by somber pines, the humble flower in these surroundings is enhanced in beauty and attracts the attention of the small gathering. Now we listen to the sound of the boiling water in the kettle, resting on a tripod over a fire in the square hole cut in the floor. The sound is not actually that of the boiling water but comes from the heavy iron kettle, and it is most appropriately likened by the connoisseur to a breeze that passes through the pine grove . . . To take a cup of tea with friends in this environment . . . lifts the mind above the perplexities of life . . . is

Teahouse at Shoren-In Temple Kyoto, Japan

it not something, indeed, to find in this world of struggles and vanities a corner, however humble, where a man can rise above the limits of relativity and even have a glimpse of eternity?[42]

Within the teahouse each element: wood, grass, fire, water, and air conspire to provoke the full symphony of the senses. Sheltering us simply in its corner, the ancient ritual possesses regenerative power precisely because its rich sensuality shifts our consciousness from rationality to reverie.

This shift in consciousness is evident in the work of Kazuyo Sejima and SANAA. At the start of her practice, Sejima wondered whether she might express the breezy, floating sensation of wearing a skirt through the medium of architecture. When describing her work, Toyo Ito said Sejima "observes intuitively the times in which she lives and diagrammatizes them directly without passing through the detours of existing conventional architectural concepts. Her medium is her own body."[43] The deceptively innocent title she chose for her 2010 Venice Bienniale exhibition, "People Meet in Architecture," reveals a philosophical position that subverts a century of architectural theory. She affirms that buildings are sensitive containers for human experience and in doing so, appeals to our broader humanity. Because her work is explicitly non-visual, it provokes conscious states beyond the strictly rational. Disarmingly ambiguous and fluid, her work has an ethereal strength. As unsettling as their apparent lack of materiality may be, her buildings have a gravitational pull that captivates. For her, curvilinear forms are not willful formal impositions but an erasure of margins, an invitation to move freshly through space. Glass is not merely transparent but a filmy veil that hints at unseen voyages.

Sejima's work points to the rich architectural potential that lies beyond vision. Rationality is exclusively identified with the visual sense, but this theory of vision is based on the scientifically and philosophically bankrupt Cartesian separation between the mind and the body. When considered as a perceptual system, the eye, the brain, and the body function together inseparably. Gibson argued that it is not the formation of a retinal image that is important to visual perception but the registering of constantly varying intensity of multi-directional light. In visual perception movement is the general case and standing still is the exception. Experimental work on visual habits demonstrates that our eyes, in a random examination of the surroundings, tend to follow flat and vertical lines. Paul Shepard speculates that our visual system has evolved from our arboreal ancestral origins:

> As we pass through a forest, the graded motion of vegetation overhead does not seem a jumble of branches and leaves: on the contrary the elaborate mesh and interlacing seem to untangle and each twig to take its proper place in space. Here too the visual world is different from a painting. A stationary observer tends to presume that all objects extend at right angles from his line of sight, as they do in a painting. But as he moves through the actual terrain the sense of being at the center of a three dimensional world falls upon him, a continuous unfolding revelation.[44]

Like a forest of rich textures and interesting overlaps, an architecture of moving vision is an adventure that continually unfolds. Highly contextual, designed for plural points of view, this architecture is not a stage set contrived for the petrified frame on a magazine cover. An unfolding architecture defies objectification, eludes capture by the eye as it discloses its secrets to those who take the time to experience them. Such is the work of sensitive perception. As the poet Mary Oliver confirms, "Of course! the path to heaven doesn't lie down in flat miles. It is in the imagination with which we perceive this world and the gestures with which we honor it."[45]

4

METAPHOR: A LOCAL HABITATION AND A NAME

*The tangible rests precariously upon
the untouched and the ungrasped.*
– John Dewey

*As imagination bodies forth
The form of things unknown, the poet's pen
Turns them into shapes, and gives to airy nothing
A local habitation and a name.*
– William Shakespeare

There is no vision without the screen.
– Maurice Merleau-Ponty

Firmly rooted in the soil of daily life, he extolled the virtues of the simple soup and visited the butcher shop in person to select the right cut of meat. He began his professional life as a postmaster in the Champagne region of France and eventually became the inaugural Chair of Philosophy at the Sorbonne. As beloved by his students as he was dearly devoted to them, Gaston Bachelard was an immensely important figure in scientific epistemology and poetics. A philosopher of science, Bachelard wrote voluminously on physics and argued that the findings of relativity and quantum mechanics had profound implications for human knowledge. He recognized that science progressed through more than the simple accumulation of facts. To prove this, he pioneered the concept of an "epistemological rupture" to describe how scientific knowledge struggles to break free from entrenched mental patterns in order to embrace new conceptual frameworks, thus anticipating Thomas Kuhn's work on paradigm shifts. Scientific breakthroughs, thought Bachelard, demonstrate the power of the imagination to penetrate beyond the reigning network of facts. In order to show that creative intelligence is a dynamic interplay between rational and imaginative capabilities, he dedicated the second half of his career exploring the source of creative knowledge.[1]

With his characteristically subversive wit, Bachelard's vast mind roamed beyond the confines of his own discipline, and for these unorthodox wanderings we are deeply indebted. From the rich storehouse of his imagination, he summoned compelling metaphors with a childlike facility. In allowing himself to peer through the "thousand windows of fantasy," he provided architects and designers with a wealth of original poetic imagery and metaphor. For Bachelard, "The poet speaks on the threshold of being."[2] This is the liminal state which, according to anthropologist Victor Turner, is the true "mother of invention".[3] At this threshold, the imagination yields its produce in the form of metaphor.

"Metaphors are not simple idealizations which take off in rockets only to display their insignificance on bursting in the sky, but on the contrary metaphors summon one another and are more coordinated than sensations, so much so that a poetic mind is purely and simply a syntax of metaphors."[4] Neuroscientists tell us that metaphors are an innate feature of our conceptual system and exemplify the uniquely human capacity to construct meaning. Metaphor essentially portrays the structure of the mind projected outwards. The Israeli poet Yehuda Amichai calls metaphor "the great human revolution, at least on par with the invention of the wheel."[5]

Because they are rooted in bodily experience, metaphors cannot be understood in absence of context or independent of their experiential basis. They spring into a fertile mind as wholes and cannot, by their very nature be reduced to their component parts. A metaphor harbors a dense web of interconnections whose meanings unravel through time. Eugene Minkowski describes the process of metaphor: "It is as though a well-spring existed in a sealed vase and its waves, repeatedly echoing against the sides of this vase, filled it with their sonority. Or again, it is as though the sound of a hunting horn, reverberating everywhere through its echo, made the tiniest leaf, the tiniest wisp of moss, shudder in common movement and transformed the whole forest, filling it to its limits, into a vibrating sonorous world."[6]

Breakthroughs in cognitive science discredit the notion that metaphor is simply a matter of language that can at best only describe reality. This view stems from the obsolete idea that what we call reality refers exclusively to the study of a physical world wholly external to and independent from the way we conceptualize that world. The "objective" view of reality dismisses the human emotions, motivations, and perceptions that literally pattern our experience in the world. In their book, *Metaphors We Live By*, Mark Johnson and George Lakoff show that metaphor is "not just a matter of language, that is, of mere words . . . Human thought processes are largely metaphorical . . . Metaphors as linguistic expressions are possible precisely because there are metaphors in a person's conceptual system."[7] Our choice of metaphor can and does powerfully shape our reality. The etymology of the word metaphor comes from the Greek *meta*, which means over and across and *pherein*, to carry to bear. *Pherein* derives from the Indo-European root *bher*, to bear, to birth. Metaphor gives birth to meaning, like raindrops in a pond whose ripples pattern significance, shape our conceptual framework, and thus determine our thoughts and actions.

Our basic concepts are generally organized around spatial categories that are rooted in our experience of being in the physical world. For example, we all share the sense that when we are happy, we are feeling upbeat. When we are sad, we feel down. When we are happy we buoyantly float on a cloud, when we are sad we sink into a pit of despair. The rational is up, while the nitty gritty of life is mundane, like crumbs that sink beneath the table. Similarly, we call a person who lacks pretense "down-to-earth". The metaphors we use mirror our shared cultural values. Our culture, for example, shares the notion that more is better and that progress is paramount; consequently we tend to expect tomorrow to be brighter. Historically much cultural change has resulted from the conceptual shifts introduced by new metaphors.

Like seeds, metaphors have entailments that germinate relative to our individual and cultural situation. They have implications through which we can highlight and organize certain aspects of our experience. Our tacitly shared metaphors not only create realities for us, they also guide our future actions. And such actions will, in turn, fit the metaphor. This of course reinforces the power of the metaphor to make sense of our experience and demonstrates the way that metaphors often become self-fulfilling prophecies.

Metaphors are not ideologically or psychologically neutral. They channel the development of our conceptual framework, opening new cognitive avenues, while simultaneously closing down and devaluing others. When choosing between conflicting theories, for example, scientists tend to select the one whose metaphor intuitively fits with their own experience. The history of science abounds with such examples. In the field of optics, the eye is understood to work like a camera, even though a fixed retinal image is the exception rather than the rule, for vision. In quantum physics, atoms are conceived to move like billiard balls bumping into each other. Perhaps the metaphor tells us more about an underlying value system, than it does to explain the behavior of the constituents of the universe.

Metaphors can be epistemic encumbrances or openings through which "the imagination bodies forth." For instance, the machine metaphor was the favored child born of Cartesian dualism. The mechanistic characterization of architecture grew out of the enthusiasm and promise of the age of industrialism. Yet the metaphor continues to permeate the conceptualization of our natural and built environment and our own bodies. Buckminster Fuller said that a person is a "self balancing 28-jointed adapter-base biped, an electro-chemical reduction plant, integral with the segregated stowages of special energy extracts in storage batteries, for subsequent actuation of thousands of hydraulic and pneumatic pumps, with motors attached . . . and a universally distributed telephone system

... *et cetera*."[8] Not surprisingly, he also famously dubbed our planet *spaceship earth*. Could there be a more anthropocentric, objectifying characterization of life?

According to the evolutionary biologist Richard Dawkins, "Each one of us is a machine, like an airliner only much more complicated."[9] Rather than mere rhetorical flourishes or devices of the poetic imagination, these metaphors pervade our daily functioning. Because our conceptual system governs our thoughts and actions in the world, our metaphors will in turn shape our surroundings. Consequently, the abstraction and mathematical reduction inherent within the mechanistic metaphor is the legacy that has rendered our current monotony of buildings.

When he coined the phrase, "The house is a machine for living in," Le Corbusier captured *l'esprit du temps* in a manner similar to Descartes. Himself a thorough Cartesian, Le Corbusier's utter fascination with the engineering feats of his day is evident in his influential book, *Towards A New Architecture*, which is packed full with images of biplanes and oceanliners. He envisioned an architecture that would match the efficiency and economy of machines. This is precisely the conceptual system that underlies the modernist movement and its major defect; airplanes are designed to fly through the air, and the oceanliner is adapted to cruise on water, but buildings are rooted in the soil, and since they do not move, they are subject to environmental relationships and limitations in a way that moving vehicles are not and should not be.

Overwhelmed with the changes ushered in by industry, Le Corbusier depicted them as a "flood which rolls on towards destined ends, [and] has furnished us with new tools adapted to this new epoch, animated by the new spirit."[10] Aligned with the progressive spirit, he suggested, "If we eliminate from our hearts and minds all dead concepts in regard to the house, and look at the question from a critical and objective point of view, we shall arrive at the House Machine the mass production house healthy (and morally too) and beautiful in the way that the working tools and instruments which accompany our existence are beautiful."[11] Le Corbusier succeeded in framing the question of the house by excising the inhabitant. Shorn of human relationships, buildings were fated to become disembodied objects on the landscape.

The machine metaphor fit the requirements of capitalism with razor sharp precision. In a milieu in which "time is money" speed and efficiency are primary values. "Out with the old and in with the new" paves the way for the "march of progress." Le Corbusier's prophecy that "cafes and places for recreation would no longer be that fungus which eats up the pavements of Paris; they would be transferred to roofs [resulting in the] triplification of traffic area of the town," is the grim reality that plagues suburbia.[12] The cruel irony is that Le Corbusier ultimately grew disillusioned with the machine and adopted organic metaphor late in his career. His most moving work is grounded in bodily and experiential interiority, a topic we will explore in Chapter Six. Modernism's embrace of the objective determinism inherent in the mechanistic ethic has eclipsed the more humane part of Le Corbusier's message, which was that, "a plan proceeds from within to without, for a house or a palace is an organism comparable to a living being."[13]

In differing ways both Jung and Einstein agreed that a problem could not be solved at the same level it was created. One of the fundamental contributions of modern architecture is the distillation of a building's form from its function. If function is the driving force of form, then a successful work of architecture is closer to an organ, than to a machine. The word organ derives the Greek *ergon* which means "work" and "energy". A machine is an object that functions with the application of external energy in a closed system. An organ functions in context with intrinsic energy, as part of an open-ended living system. An organ is not a thing, it is a living relationship. Relationship defines everything that is alive. Only that which is not alive can be conceived of as a complicated set of parts. Clearly architecture and machines are both human artifacts, but the key difference is that we live *in* the material presence of a building, which is then rooted in varying degrees in its environmental context. The materiality of a building is coextensive with its surroundings, it is a *viniculum substantiale*, to use Merleau-Ponty's terminology, or the phenomenal partner in "flexible consubstantiality", to use Victor Hugo's.[14] From this mutual perspective, a building is not an object, a thing in itself, at all.

Rather, a building more closely resembles a living system in which information is processed via countless cascading feedback loops, whose implications, like Minkowski's prismatic description of metaphor, reverberate everywhere and make "the tiniest wisp of moss shudder in common movement and transformed the whole forest, filling it to its limits, into a vibrating sonorous world." Information conceived mechanistically does not possess such open-ended entailments. But as the architect Charles Jencks writes, "Surprisingly, many architects today give up aesthetic responsibility and hide behind cost, function, planning requirements, or some other alibi . . . Architects have the freedom to choose metaphor and form language, indeed they have an obligation to do so, it is virtually their most open choice."[15]

The human achievement in projecting "subjective impulses into institutional forms, aesthetic symbols, mechanical organizations, and architectural structures have been vastly augmented by the orderly cooperative methods that science has exemplified and universalized," wrote Lewis Mumford. "But at the same time, to reduce acceptable subjectivity to the ideal level of a computer would only sever rationality and order from their own deepest sources in the organism. If we are to save technology itself . . . we must in both in our thinking and acting, come back to the human center."[16] In his book, *Imagination and the Meaningful Brain*, the psychiatrist Arnold Modell argues that, "Human experience cannot be omitted from a scientific explanation of how the mind/brain works."[17] Because different domains of the mind function differently, the rules that govern one part of the brain do not necessarily apply to others. Algorithms that describe activity in the visual cortex, for example, do not explain fantasy and our ability to imagine our own internal reality. "The construction of meaning is not the same as the processing of information; meaning cannot be 'represented' by a formal symbolic code."[18] Metaphors are the cognitive expression of our lived experience in the world. They do not *represent* reality, they embody our uniquely enriched, imaginative reality. Metaphor is a defining characteristic of our humanity, their careful choice can celebrate human experience.

As Bachelard pointed out, the parallel histories of architecture and science progress through the collective capacity of the imagination to reach beyond the reigning accumulation of facts. The neuroscientists who discovered mirror neurons in Parma, Italy, for instance, were able to overcome the limitations of the prevailing paradigm because they maintained an open-minded approach to their empirical evidence. Practicing epistemic pluralism, neurophysiologist Vittorio Gallese searched beyond the strict confines of his discipline, and found analogies and images in Merleau-Ponty's work that enabled him to coherently formulate his discovery.[19] Bridging the reasoning and imaginative faculties of the mind, metaphors bind together experimental results that are otherwise incomprehensible.

Similarly, when Sejima wondered whether the medium of architecture could express the sensation of a skirt brushing across her legs, she circumvented the conventional repertoire of architectural metaphor. Charged with life-force and generative capacity, hers is a metaphor that embodies the process through which we house the untouched and ungrasped.

PRACTICALLY UNCONSCIOUS

Doubt is an uncomfortable condition,
but certainty is a ridiculous one.
– Voltaire

Uncertainty is primarily a practical matter.
– John Dewey

Id means *it*. Freud borrowed his term for the unconscious from Latin. *It* was his alien sump of repressed desires and animal instincts whose domestication is Civilization's mandate. The prefix *id* crops up in many English words: it underlies the aspirations of our highest *ide*als, when we're wasting time we are *id*le, we worship *id*ols, we call a person who is "incapable of ordinary reasoning" an *id*iot, and our individual uniqueness our *id*entity. It is not surprising, given our cultural emphasis on reason and determinism, that something as elusive and pervasive as the unconscious provokes such profound ambivalence. The words, idle, ideal, idol, express an interesting contradiction: the first means empty and the second two both connote a container like form. An ideal contains our thoughts while an idol is a vessel into which we pour our hidden hopes and desires. Lao Tzu expresses the functional interdependence between container and contained in his poem:

> Thirty spokes share the wheel's hub;
> it is the center hole which makes it useful.
> Shape the clay into a vessel;
> It is the space inside that makes it useful.
> Cut doors and windows for a room;
> It is the hole which makes it useful.
> Therefore profit comes from what is there,
> usefulness comes from what is not there.[1]

Cognitive scientists would most likely agree that when it comes to consciousness, "usefulness comes from what is not there." For they tell us that the unconscious, which they call the 'cognitive unconscious', comprises 95% of our total cognitive functioning. And they admit that even this may be a serious underestimate. All conceptions of cognitive science are based on the finding that our thoughts take shape through cognitive structures of which we are largely unconscious. We simply do not have direct conscious awareness of what occurs in our minds. Paul Valery described it thus: "Our simplest act, our most familiar gesture, could not be performed, the least of our powers might become an obstacle to us, if we had to bring it before the mind and know it thoroughly in order to exercise it."[2] In a conversation, we are not only listening to the words being said, we are looking at facial and other bodily gestures, measuring the duration of pauses, deciding what to say next, tensing our jaws, feeling our tummies grumble, thinking about last night's dinner, noticing our uncomfortable chair and on and on. In short, infinitely more is impressed upon our minds than we can ever attend to or perceive.

The complexity of such a daily occurrence has remarkable implications. For most of its history, Western philosophy has considered itself independent of empirical investigation. Philosophers have staunchly clung to the theory that they could peer into their own minds to understand their functioning, a condition epitomized in the Cartesian dictum: "I think, therefore I am." Though we know very little about what actually takes place in our minds, we do know that if the cognitive unconscious were not doing the shaping, there would be no conscious thought. Thinking is but one facet of being—necessary, but not sufficient to define us. This completely reverses Descartes' premise. Until relatively recently, conscious reasoning was considered the executive control system of the mind. But the assumption of classical rationalism—that reason is independent of perception and bodily movement—is incorrect. This view was formed prior to evolutionary theory, which clearly proves that human capacities emerge out of animal capacities. Human reason exists on a continuum with animal reason and is hitched inextricably to our bodies and brains. Consciousness is shaped by the biological, chemical, and electrical details of our embodiment in interaction with our environment.

Our thoughts are implicitly molded by our bodily experience in place. We cannot overestimate the extent to which our environment silently and constantly shapes us. To accept the force of this reality contradicts the entrenched Western notion that humans exist in complete independence of their surroundings. In reducing a person to an isolated, purely rational agent, we've underestimated his sensitivity, stripped him of his vulnerability, and ultimately robbed him of his humanity. In his study, *The Unconscious Before Freud*, Lancelot Law Whyte writes:

> The European and Western ideal of the self aware individual confronting destiny with his own indomitable will and skeptical reason as the only factors on which he can rely is perhaps the noblest aim which has yet been accepted by any community . . . But it has become evident that this ideal was a moral mistake and an intellectual error, for it has exaggerated the ethical, philosophical, and scientific importance of the awareness of the individual. And one

of the main factors exposing this inadequate ideal is the rediscovery of the unconscious mind. That is why the *idea of the unconscious is the supreme revolutionary concept of the modern age.*[3]

Long before the advent of cognitive science, psychologists and philosophers in the nineteenth century recognized that the concept of the unconscious was necessary to understand certain aspects of human experience and behavior. But the Cartesian/Freudian image of the unconscious as the subversive sump tank of the mind remains essentially unchallenged, even today. We persist in believing that human identity derives solely from our conscious intelligence, a position proven to be both scientifically and philosophically erroneous. Conscious intelligence grows out of and is structured by the unconscious. But because we understand consciousness to be controlled and rational, we assume that its corollary, the unconscious to be wild and chaotic. The images of the unconscious that continue to resurface in contemporary culture are further renditions of the solipsistic man who faces his destiny armed only with his 'indomitable will'.

Consciousness remains an insoluable riddle as long as we insist on explaining it in terms of itself. We can only understand consciousness in relation to the unconscious. Failing to accept this essential interdependence locks us into exclusive reliance on the modes of knowing that are preeminently associated with the conscious mind. Yet as William James affirms, "Our normal waking consciousness, rational consciousness as we call it, is but one type of special consciousness, whilst all about it, parted from it by the filmiest of screens, there lie potential forms of consciousness entirely different . . . No account of the universe in its totality can be final which leaves these other forms of consciousness quite disregarded."[4]

We need to affirm the mystery while dispelling the horror of the unconscious. The philosopher Leibnitz did not characterize the unconscious as the terrifying *Id*, but as the better part of an iceberg that underlies conscious thought. The iceberg metaphor reconciled his two ideas about the unconscious that continue to endure today. First, that consciousness and unconsciousness share a continuum and second that a threshold lies between consciousness and unconsciousness, over which only a thought with a certain amount of charge can traverse. He said, "Our clear concepts are like islands that rise above the ocean of obscure ones."[5] The unconscious continues to be popularly characterized as an iceberg, our clear thoughts sit atop a submerged mass of immense proportion, and like a hidden hand, the massive invisible portion of the iceberg shapes conscious thought.

Thought is inherently contextual, so naturally Leibnitz's metaphor evolved from his situation in a Northern climate, one in which he may have been exposed to the phenomena of icebergs. But the iceberg is inadequate to describe the function of the unconscious. Not only is it a sterile, frigid, and an isolated object, it is barren and inert. While icebergs harbor burgeoning life about their perimeter, they actually scrape and gouge the ocean floor and destroy life below them. Perhaps if he had lived near the equator, the image of a more vital island might have captured his imagination.

Islands that bridge land and sea, mangroves are one of the earth's most complex ecosystems and robust carbon sinks. They "have a life force strong enough to alter the visible face of their world," writes Linda Hogan.[6] Mangroves are tidal forests brilliantly adapted to thrive in an inundated toxic environment that would prove fatal to most other plants. Through their massive network of capillaries they function as giant lungs that filter pollution, protect coastlines from erosion and dissipate the destructive waves of hurricanes and tsunamis. While their heads stick out above the water, the bulk of their tremendous presence is invisible to the eye, sunken below the water's surface, rooted to the sea floor, silently nourishing diverse life forms. Their tangle of roots intercepts sediment and digests decaying leaves to form new coastlines. Migratory birds as far north as Maine depend on the narrow fringe of mangrove in Mexico and Central America for nesting, habitat, and foraging. Mangroves on the Pacific coast host eighty percent of the migratory bird populations in North America. Though mangroves may nurture the ongoing creation and renewal of the world, over half of the world's mangrove forests have been destroyed in recent times. We fail to understand that our lives in some way depend on their health and vitality. As Freud did with the *Id*, we objectify in order to control.

21st Century Museum, Kanasawa, Japan, SANAA

Mangrove in Belize

In the 19th century William James suggested that consciousness should be understood as a process, not an object. Why not portray the continuum of consciousness as an intricately balanced web work at once rooted to the earth, subject to fluctuating tides, capable of absorbing shocks and toxins while nursing new life, enlarging boundaries, and constantly renewing our vitality? Our conscious thought truly emerges from the rich loam of the unconscious. This view of the unconscious portrays our identity as embedded and resumed in a greater whole. Since we know that what is visible and conscious emerges from a vast source, shouldn't we then design to appeal to the full dignity of a person who not only thinks, but feels and sleeps and dreams and imagines? Instead, our contemporary built environment was designed for the classical rationalist and dutiful consumer.

If we close our eyes, take a deep breath, and summon meaningful memories, we quickly notice that they are tied to a specific place. The place evokes a network of sensations, the warmth of sunlight on your skin, the smell of your love, the sound of her voice. Architecture, through its unique means, creates a harbor for these ephemeral, tangible things. As Bachelard said, "The house is one of the greatest powers of integration for the thoughts, memories, and dreams of mankind."[7] Like the metaphors we choose, architecture can provide a horizon, a safe harbor to the boundlessness of our unconscious. The following passage suggests such a possibility: "My house is diaphanous, but it is not of glass. It is more the nature of vapor. Its walls contract and expand as I desire. At times, I draw them close about me like protective armor . . . but at others, I let the walls of my house blossom out in their own space, which is infinitely extensible."[8]

At the 2010 Venice Bienniale, Transsolar and Tenzo Kondo collaborated to create a Cloudscape. Within an innocuous chamber

Cloudscape, Tenzo Kendo and Transsolar

of the Arsenale, they suspended a spiral ramp inside a stratiform cloud. The ramp, though thin and aging in rust, offers comforting solidity; when you ascend it, you exhale your own moist air and inhale the cloud vapor. Your internal world fuses with designed reality, bridged by the breath. The vapor of a cloud is directionless and forever moving, so subtle we forget that it is material. But a cloud is basically a family of water droplets tethered to earth by gravity. Long a symbol of the unconscious mind, water is ocean, lake, stream, and mist. When water droplets get heavy enough they gather together inside the cloud and fall to earth as raindrops or snowflakes. And so it is with our minds, when saturated in the bath of the unconscious, thoughts, memories, forms, and metaphors tumble into consciousness.

Memories are saturated with bodily connotations and resonances, perhaps nothing triggers memory more than scent. As Proust memorialized in *Remembrance of Things Past*, "When nothing else subsists from the past, after the people are dead, after the things are broken or scattered the smell and taste of things remain poised a long time, like souls, bearing resiliently, on tiny, almost impalpable drops of their essence, the immense edifice of memory."[9] Unlike color which "always remains the prisoner of an enclosing form; by contrast, the smell of an object always escapes."[10] Scent is the vapor cloud broadcast by someone's body. The olfactory sense that comprises smell and taste is our most primitive and intimate sense.[11]

Though the antiseptic quality of most contemporary spaces is impotent to provoke memory, there are some notable exceptions. Richard Serra's *Torqued Ellipses* at the DIA: Beacon in New York is a set of hull-like forms of steel alive in the process of rusting. Designed to be entered, when you move inside the curves, you can smell the acidic rust brush against your peripersonal space.[12] You sense compression tingle inside your nose as the hard shapes wrap around you. It feels like being enveloped in an immense body. Serra said that what interests him "is an opportunity for all of us to become something different from what we are, by constructing spaces that contribute something to the experience of who we are."[13] His sculpture succeeds in arousing memory precisely because it is so sensually provocative.

A shift in our experience enriches who we are. When an animal detects and then responds to a new smell, for example, there is a corresponding change in all other brain patterns.[14] Patterns of activity in the brain constantly dissolve, reform, and shift in relation to one another. Ripples of association spread out and enrich the matrix of meaning. John Dewey said that memory means that ev-

Torqued Ellipses, Richard Serra

ery experience absorbs something from those that have gone before and changes the quality of those that come after. Our bodies, unlike our computers, house no fixed representations, but only meanings. Dwelling in a forest or a vibrant city is a sensual feast. Our perceptions in such sensory enriched contexts are shot through with greater significance because felt meaning is embodied. When we sense something deeply, we are physically affected, we become "marked by nature". The warp of meaning woven into the fabric of experience consists of these bodily suggestions. Michael Ondaatje beautifully expresses this intertwining:

We die containing a richness of lovers and tribes, tastes we have swallowed, bodies we have plunged into and swum up as if rivers of wisdom, characters we have climbed into as if trees, fears we have hidden in as if caves. I wish for all of this to be marked on my body when I am dead. I believe in such cartography—to be marked by nature, not just to label ourselves on a map like the names of rich men and women on buildings. We are communal histories, communal books. We are not owned or monogamous in our taste or experience. All I desired was to walk upon such an earth that had no maps.[15]

Moments like debris awash in a flood of memory are intercepted in the web of the unconscious and eventually knit back into consciousness anew. Remembering and imagining draw on the same neural pathways, and are more similar than we realize.[16] Memories, dreams, and our imagination are linked inextricably with the objects of our lives and the rich associations we have with meaningful places. But in our culture's steadfast dedication to consumption and built-in obscelence, we no longer mend, we discard. Objects of meaning are replaced with disposable products. As architects and builders of the manifest world, our project is to "facilitate man's homecoming," as Aldo Van Eyck reminds us.[17]

Home is for Bachelard a shelter for our dreams. Like a mangrove whose submerged invisible strands nurture new land forms, our dreams flow nightly in the transformed consciousness of sleep. We spend roughly thirty percent of our lives sleeping, but sleep remains a mystery. Sponge-like in the way it absorbs the shocking waves of daily life, sleep is elastic in its capacity to renew us at the break of the day. "Our intense need was absorbed by the night and returned as sustenance," writes the poet Louise Gluck.[18] Despite the fact that our need to sleep is so basic, millions of people suffer from insomnia. We are so busy legitimizing our existence during the day that it becomes impossible to turn the lights out at night. If we can't even sleep, how are we supposed to dream? We resent the need to sleep. Yet our common sense knows that the best solution to a problem is revealed to us after we 'sleep on it'.

Dreaming is essential to a full creative life. "For he who dreams not creates not, for vapor must rise into the air before rain can fall."[19] The Japanese have the word, *myo*, that is does not translate into English. Similar to dreaming and imagining, *myo* is a quality that originates in one's unconscious. No amount of training can substitute for the gracious appearance of *myo*. D.T. Suzuki describes it as a:

> certain artistic quality perceivable not only in works of art but in anything in Nature or life. The sword in the hands of the swordsman attains this quality when it is not a mere display of technical skill patiently learned under the tutorship of a good master . . . The hands may move according to the technique given out to every student, but there is a certain spontaneity and personal creativity when the technique, conceptualized, and universalized, is handled by the master hand. *Myo* may also be applied to the intelligence and the instinctive activities of various animals, for example the beaver building its nest, the spider spinning its web, the wasp or ant constructing its castles under the eaves or beneath the ground. They are the wonders of Nature. In fact, the whole universe is a miraculous exhibition of a master mind, and we humans who are one of its wonderful achievements have been straining our intellectual efforts ever since the awakening of consciousness and are daily being overwhelmed by Nature's demonstrations of its unfathomable and inexhaustible *myoyu*. The awakening of consciousness has been the greatest cosmological event in the course of evolution. We have been able by its practical application to probe into the secrets of nature and make use of them to serve our way of living, but at the same time we seem to be losing the many things we have otherwise been enjoying

which Nature has been liberal enough to grant us. The function
of human consciousness, as I see it, is to dive deeper and deeper
into its source, the unconscious.[20]

The Haiku poem is one vehicle for *myo*. Haiku short-circuits the intellect and dips directly into the unconscious. Basho writes,

> The old pond, ah!
> A frog jumps in:
> The water's sound![21]

It is not through the stillness of the pond that the poet experiences the unconscious. It is through the sound stirred by the frog's
leap. The haiku convinces not through ideas or concepts, but
through familiar incident, a sensory event, crowned by the gasp of
astonishment. We share our unconscious with animals and with
each other. The unconscious underlies every simple gesture and
communication that we take for granted. It is the source of the
unpredictable, unexplainable, ordinary mystery that we encounter
in each moment. Our buildings not only shelter our bodies, they
can be a substrate that nurtures our imagination. Like a haiku poem,
we can short-circuit the intellect. Stir up memories, invite touch,
introduce heat, make something so beautiful that we want to eat it.
Create comfort so luscious we can stop thinking and start dreaming.

6

DARK MATTERS

. . . then, I looked down and saw the world I was entering,
that would be my home. And I turned to my companion and said,
where are we? And he replied, Nirvana
And I said again, but the light will give us no peace."

– Louise Gluck

Night's shadow softens gradually. The sun's first luminous rays reach across time bending over the earth's smooth curve, faltering at first, then growing wide and constant, stabilizing like the broad blue at the base of a flame. The transition is certain, the daily shift from dark to light announced by a band of blue, the moment of tranquility, when the silence of night is thrilled by life awakened. This is the "blue hour" between darkness and daylight when flowers are at their most fragrant and when creatures rustle, fly up, and trade places. It is the term the French biologist Jean-Henri Fabre used to describe the moment when nocturnal animals fall asleep and diurnal ones awaken. He said, "Nearly all animals on earth greet night in this moment of blue, find slumber in it, and awaken to it day after day."[1] Scientists have discovered that the human eye contains a novel photoreceptor uniquely sensitive to the blue/violet wavelengths of the light spectrum.[2] Our eyes are designed not just for seeing; our retina also contains non-cone, non-rod receptors that absorb twilight, signaling our brain to entrain with the oscil-

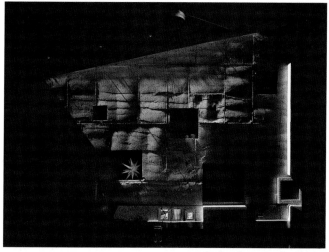

Catalina House, Interior, Rick Joy

Light spectrum and relative lengths of color cones in our eyes

lations of the light and dark cycle. Merleau-Ponty would delight in this discovery. For he speculated that the only 'place' we could find the negative would be at the fold.[3] Twilight, the band of blue, is one such fold. Young in its fragility and ancient in its regenerative presence, the folded light at dawn cues our bodies to shift cycles, to tune into day.

In our modern lives, our eyes seem to be more attuned to the blue of our computer and television monitors, than the azure at twilight. As architects, we are obsessed with light. Light from every direction, natural and artificial, we can't get enough of it. The steel-framed, glass box is the quintessent triumph of our conquest of light. Louis Kahn's saying that "The sun never knew how wonderful it was until it fell on the wall of a building," seems an understatement. Our very power lies in our ability to flood spaces with light's redemption. All life depends on sunlight; our technological lives are literally fueled by its primeval distillation. Though ubiquitous, we take the presence of light for granted. Yet light is elusive. Because we can see it, we think we know it. Without light we could not see, but we *cannot* actually see light. Instead, we see light's reflection, the way in which something is illuminated. The way light is cast onto form informs us about shapes and substance. Light depends on material objects, just as the objects depend on light to be seen.

Jun'ichirō Tanizaki understands this profound interdependence. In his classic essay, *In Praise of Shadows*, he writes, "Such is our way of thinking—we find beauty not in the thing itself but in the patterns of shadows, the light and the darkness, the one thing against another creates."[4] Not fully beautiful in isolation, objects gain their character by virtue of the variables in which they are situated. "The sheen of the lacquer, set out in the night, reflects the wavering candlelight, announcing the drafts that find their way from time to time into the quiet room, luring one into a state of reverie. If the lacquer is taken away, much of the spell disappears from the dream world built by the strange light of candle and lamp, that wavering light bearing the pulse of the night. Indeed the thin, impalpable, faltering light, picked up as though little rivers were running through the room, collecting little pools here and there, lacquers a pattern on the surface of night itself."[5] Rivulets of light that bear the pulse of night: such subtlety is missing from our under-dimensioned Western spaces. Our overwhelmingly one-sided quest for light is a manifestation of our Enlightenment rationality, but our souls and even our eyes long for shadows.

We fail to appreciate that light actually contains darkness. The wavelengths recognizable as color to the human eye form only a sliver of the entire electromagnetic spectrum. As vibratory wave phenomena, sound contains silence, just as light contains darkness. When you clap your hands to make a rhythm, for example, there is a silence between the claps. It is precisely this silence that enables you to distinguish the sounds. Speed up the clapping and the vibration turns into a tone. These tones, like light waves involve an alternation between sound and silence. Paul Valery said, "The secret of the blackness of milk is accessible only through its whiteness."[6] This is analogous to Merleau-Ponty's observation that silence envelopes language. We can only see the brilliance of stars against the darkness of sky. In our love of light, we must praise the night. The existence of one is wholly contingent upon the other. Yet a synthesis of light and dark makes a murky gray. Allowing each it's own integrity expresses the contradiction which lies at the heart of truly poetic work. As Basho writes:

Oh detestable crow
today alone
you please me
black against
The snow [7]

In *Mind as Nature*, Loren Eiseley wrote, "The mind has a latent, lurking fertility, not unrelated to the Universe from which it sprang."[8] In truth the galaxy we inhabit spirals in a sea of darkness. Scientists speculate that ninety-six percent of all matter is dark matter. The percentage of dark matter in space strangely parallels the percentage of the unconscious that cognitive scientists estimate to comprise cognition. Perhaps our idolization of light is directly proportional to our fear of the dark. In a popular Persian tale, the revered Mulla Nasrudin knelt down on his hands and knees and was busily groping around in the dirt in front of his house, when his passing friend asked him what he was doing. The exasperated Mulla replied, "My buttons . . . my buttons, I have lost my buttons." His friend asked, "Where did you lose them, Mulla?" "Back there in my house," said Nasrudin, who angrily pointed at his house. "Well then . . . why do you search here?" asked the perplexed friend. The Mulla answered, "Because the light is so much better here." When astronomers ceased searching the heavens for light and turned their attention to empirical matters, they discovered dark matter and dark energy. The relatively recent discovery of dark matter in space caused controversy and puzzlement, but coming to terms with its pervasive presence has inspired an entirely new theory of the cosmos.

One of the most startling and enigmatic constituents of the universe, dark matter neither emits nor absorbs light. Its composition is unknown, yet it shapes structure, forms galaxies, and will ultimately determine the fate of the universe. According to cosmologists

Paul Steinhardt and Neil Turok, "We owe our existence to dark matter."[9] Its discovery enhances our understanding of the universe on both the smallest and largest scales imaginable. Their book, *Endless Universe*, unveils the cyclic model of the universe, the theory that stands to potentially embarrass the reigning big bang theory. The cyclic model was inspired by dark energy and dark matter and is consistent with quantum physics, unified field theories, and the string theory. It describes an evolving universe "in which galaxies, stars and life have been formed over and over again long before the most recent big bang and will be remade cycle after cycle far into the future."[10] It reveals the notion of the beginning of time to be a hubristic and unproven assumption. The authors contend that the cyclic understanding of the universe "should open one's mind to the possibility of evolutionary time scales that are far greater than ever imagined . . . This is perhaps one of the most important 'new' ideas to emerge from the cyclic picture."[11] The transformation in thinking provoked by the discovery of dark matter has turned out to solve numerous cosmological puzzles.

As architects it is also our task to be empirically responsible. Inspired by the daring of scientists from cosmologists to cognitive scientists, we too should plunge into the nocturnal abyss. We will be in good company. Renzo Piano has compared architecture to seeing in the dark: "You know that if you look into the dark for long enough, after awhile you begin to make out things that you would not be able to see if you did not peer at them obstinately."[12] The Ute Indians of North America believe that the secret of life dwells not in the open sun but in the shadows. To really see something you must look deeply into the shadow of a living thing and for this, we see without our eyes. Decades ago Rilke declared that the work of the eye is done. Indeed, stepping into the dark activates our non-visual senses. Perhaps exploring the possibilities of awareness availed through our non-sighted senses might loosen the unrelenting grip that vision continues to exert over our culture's social, intellectual, and aesthetic life.

Our ears orient us to a multidimensional world beyond that which lies directly in front of us. The fluid-filled circular canals of our inner ear enable us to stand up straight because the motion of fluid and calcium crystals against the hair-tipped sensing cells within the canals of the ear define the motion of the head and its relationship to the earth's field of gravity. This sophisticated and delicate sense helps us to stand straight *and* think straight. The vestibular system is richly interwoven with the brain circuitry of the other senses, especially that of sight, hearing, and various feeling senses. Our sonar system permits us to "see" with our eyes closed, accessing modes of consciousness to which we may not be typically accustomed. For, as the poet Borges asks, "Who can know himself more than the blind man?"

The darkness deep inside caves is home to our earliest paintings. The oldest, such as those at Lascaux, France, were painted over thirty thousand years ago. Accessing these paintings requires a long, arduous, torch-lit journey, and makes one wonder why they are located so deeply within the caves and how this affects their meaning. Research reveals that in the locations where ungulates—the hoofed animals of the sort probably hunted by these people—are pictured, the acoustics are extraordinarily resonant, whereas the locations where feline animals are depicted have very little resonance. The artists may have purposely sought out the highly resonant cavities for chanting, drumming, or some sort of percussive sound that would sanctify their hunt. Perhaps the echoes represented the sound the hooves make when the animals were running, and indeed these animals are depicted in motion. Maybe the echoes set the vibratory stage for the manifestation of a successful hunt. As the composer Murray Schafer divined, "When architectural historians begin to realize that most ancient buildings were constructed not so much to enclose space as to enshrine sound, a new era in the subject will open out."[13]

Chthonic themes were pivotal in Le Corbusier's most influential post-mechanistic works. He worked on the Catholic complex of Sainte Baume over a period of fifteen years, the time span during which Le Chapel Du Ronchamp and Sainte Marie de la Tourette were completed. Le Corbusier's profound affection for the site, client, and program are evident in his correspondence. He wrote, "We are at Sainte Baume in Provence, the sacred plateau, the high place dedicated to the Saint Mary Magdalene. Centuries of faith … One would like to think, collect oneself, meditate. For years Trouin and I had prepared a major awakening—architectural and icono-graphical—for La Sainte Baume: underground basilica, mystery and twilight … and outside, people living in genuine simplicity to the scale of the landscape, the scale of their gestures and their hearts. It was beautiful."[14] Through awakening qualities latent in the place, Le Corbusier wanted to summon the spirit of Mary Magdalene and link her with local primal deities. His design involved tunneling into the earth to create passageways that connected subterranean chambers. Once submerged, visitors entered a cavity that was the dwelling place of the saint. The cave symbolized the interior of Mary Magda-lene's body and the surrounding landscape was to be sculpted into a park that represented her extended self: "For chest, central leafy pla-teau, for buttock and suggestion of thigh the Eastern plateau."[15] This fusion of building and landscape was intended to engage visitors as true participants in an erotic/spiritual communion with the saint.

Light, color, sound, and rhythm were elements Le Corbusier used to provoke a visceral experience on the journey of initiation. The passage into the earth was orchestrated to climax the moment one was ushered out to the shimmering luminosity of the Mediterrean Sea. Though this project remained unbuilt, the design process proved seminal. The two other commissions for the Catholic Church that he completed during Sainte-Baume's duration bear the imprint of the deep interiority and sensuality embodied in the design.

Peter Zumthor, the 2009 recipient of the Pritzker Prize, brilliantly crafted a contemporary cave in Vals, Switzerland. Not unlike St. Baume, one enters the thermal baths through a mysteriously dark tunnel that pierces the earth. The passage pauses at a gallery to permit a panorama of baths below. Ensconced in stratified stone, the baths seem to have been carved by time, rather than constructed with the hand. Light enters the cavernous interior through edges of glass that have been embedded in the stone with great precision. The massive stone walls are rinsed with light, evanescent, it reflects off of mica and quartz and refracts upon the shifting presence of water. Water is everywhere. Naked bodies are dignified in shrouds of steam. The steamy mist, rather than being a contrivance, is generated naturally from below the earth's crust. One swims through mist-clouded water, which is framed by the jagged profile of the high Alps.

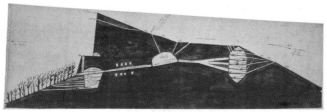

Cross Section of Sainte Baume, Le Corbusier

Zumthor feels that architecture has a special physical relationship with life. He says, "I do not think of it primarily as either message or symbol, but as an envelope and background for life which goes on in and around it, a sensitive container for the rhythm of footsteps on the floor, for the construction of work, for the silence of sleep."[16]

Feeling our way in the dark refines our senses, helps us recognize opportunities we may have otherwise missed and opens uncharted terrain. To gain inspiration, the composer Brian Eno holes up in a strange place with no stimulation and nothing to rely on except the 'the horror of his own company.' And eventually as if from nowhere, the creative spark crackles. "It's like jumping into the abyss and discovering that you can just drift dreamily on air currents," he muses.[17] The mystic Meister Eckhart said that the ground of the soul is dark. Cosmologists tell us that it is darkness we float upon. We now know that this essential darkness underlies all of life, a fact which poets of all ages have long known.

DARK MATTERS

You, darkness, of whom I am born—
I love you more that the flame
That limits the world
In the circle it illumines
And excludes all of the rest.

But the dark embraces everything:
Shapes and shadows, creatures and me,
People, nations—just as they are.

It lets me imagine
A great presence stirring beside me.

I believe in the night.

– Rainer Maria Rilke

TIME IS RHYTHM

The moon is a mirror of time.
– Persian metaphor

I want to be a mirror for your whole body.
– Rainer Maria Rilke

Our architecture reflects us, as truly as a mirror,
even if we consider it apart from us.
– Louis Sullivan

Whenever I go to Phoenix I get lost. Before the economy crashed it was the fastest growing city in North America. It looks like it was built in a day and such a monoscape makes way-finding difficult. But when driving one day, I did find one landmark that erupted from the metastasis of strip malls and drive-thru fast food chains. It was an enormous billboard in bumble bee black with yellow letters that read, "Bankruptcy and Divorce, 300$". A roadside invitation to erase the past. This primary colored emblem was inseparable from its surroundings and their logical consequence: disposal is the destiny of mistaking the pursuit of happiness for the freedom to consume. The promise of a quick bailout typifies the "born again" syndrome that is so prevalent in Western culture. Edward T. Hall noticed that, "Whenever anything new is adopted—a belief, a lifestyle or even a spouse—there are deep unconscious patterns that make us feel we must disavow the old. In disavowing our past, we fragment history and in the process manage to break the few remaining threads that bind, stabilize, and give unity to life."[1]

The rigid division of past from present and the guarantee of a brighter future, characterize the Western concept of time. For us, time is a commodity, like money. We save it, spend it, waste it, but mostly, as if it were a shopping cart, we are compelled to fill it. Time lacks personality; it is neutral, unrelenting, and anxious. "Time waits for no man", which is perhaps why we find it so easy to "kill" time. The concept of time as an objectively existing entity is necessary to the smooth operation of a clockwork universe. Isaac Newton formulated "absolute, true, and mathematical time, [which] of itself and from its own nature flows equally without regard to anything external."[2] But the notion that time is a distinct container whose fulfillment depends on our enterprise and industry, is alien to most non-Western cultures.

For pre-industrial people, time is not isolated from place or from ourselves; it is more like a stream that we are in—a relational concept that can be understood only in terms of other concepts such as space, motion, or events. Physicists no longer refer to time in and of itself, but to space-time, which they say can stretch, contract, warp, or wiggle. Most human languages share the notion that time moves, and that it is defined by successive events. Neither static nor immutable, time does not have an independent existence. This meaning is embedded in the English word *time*, which derives from the word *tide*. Both words mean constant motion and duration. Tidal motion highlights the cyclic dimension of time. Unlike the Western concept of time, with its discrete beginning and fatal end, for Native Americans time is an eternally recurring cycle of events and years. Some of their languages lack terms to indicate the past and the future because both are enveloped in the present.

A Persian metaphor says that the moon is a mirror of time.[3] The quiet moon controls the tidal motions of our oceans. Reflecting the sun's light, lunar waxing and waning situates us in a galaxy of flux and continuity. The shaded moon traces cyclic time, we find comfort in the moon's constant, yet ever changing presence. Marking the border between our earth and intergalactic space, our kinship with the moon is strongest in the eclipse. When our trajectories align, we cast our shadow on her face. The moon's gravitation tugs the earth's conducting liquids, including the fluids in our own bodies. The gestation and egg-hatching of many animals and the human menstrual cycle are tuned to lunar timing. Tidal forces generate currents in the earth's interior that affect its magnetic field.

When Whitman remarked that "nature neither hastens nor delays", he was referring to *tidal*, cyclic time not clock time. In cyclic time we inhabit vast cosmic cycles in which the passage of time heals. We nourish the promise of regeneration when we participate in time's flow. Early humans precisely charted the sun's movement along the horizon, and synchronized their activities with the natural cycles of light and dark. Evidence suggests that the Cro-Magnons had begun to make and record systematic observations of moon phases, animal migrations, the spawning of salmon.[4] Such knowledge certainly enhanced their chances for survival. The sun's passage determined the dates for planting, harvesting, and festivals. The first structures made by humans were built precisely for this purpose: Stonehenge, New Grange, and other observatories sited at thousands of places around the globe laid the foundation for modern science. We can say that the rhythmic oscillation between lightness and darkness is one of the original impulses generating architecture.

In the 18th century, the botanist Carl Linneaus noticed that the flowers of many plants open and close periodically at times that varied according to their species. He hypothesized that one could create a flower clock by arranging different flowers that opened sequentially over the course of a day.[5] This periodic opening and closing is brought about by the interaction of an internally generated rhythm and day length. The gradual transition from dark to light is our situation of living on a rotating planet. We share physiological, biochemical, and behavioral processes with all plants and animals that are cued to the changing light levels. We exist in these rhythms. Synchronization with the cycles of darkness and light is a fundamental characteristic of all living beings. The very essence of time is rhythm because equal intervals of time define a succession of events as rhythmic.

The term *circadian* was invented to describe the entrainment that occurs between our internally generated rhythm and the daily cycles of light. The science of chronobiology studies the daily, tidal, and seasonal rhythms in living beings. Circadian rhythms cue long term processes such as migration, hibernation, and endocrine levels that in turn trigger fattening and fur growth. These processes are tuned months in advance to day length. This "body clock" is deeply entrenched in our makeup. Circadian timing is not an emergent characteristic of the brain but an integral feature in the biochemistry of our cells. Linneaus imagined his clock of flowers. Ours is a calendar of delicately shifting endocrine levels.

Endocrine disruption is an important issue researched by the National Institute of Environmental Health Sciences. In contemporary life we spend most of our time indoors, and consequently receive on average less than two hours of sunlight per day.[6] Prior to industrialization, humans experienced dark nights and bright, broad-spectrum days. Unlike artificial light, sunlight varies in intensity, spectral content and timing over the course of a day. Evidence clearly indicates that light for vision and light for circadian function are utterly different.[7] Yet electric lighting in buildings is designed for visual performance and not for the maintenance of endocrine rhythms. Because we get insufficient light during the day and too much light at night, artificial lighting in its current application contributes to circadian disruption, which may be an important cause of endocrine disruption and thereby contribute to a high risk of breast cancer, infertility, and sleep disorders in industrialized societies.[8]

In *Art and Experience* John Dewey wrote, "A common interest in rhythm is still the tie which holds science and art in kinship."[9] Human periodicities are nested within concentrically larger social and cosmic periodicities. Dewey believed that rhythms underlie all of the arts from painting and sculpture, architecture, to music, dance, and literature. Rhythm is basic to synchrony and resonance, the tie which binds music and architecture, a subject we explored as we bid adieu to Descartes. The wave phenomena of light can be expressed in a scale like that of music. A rhythm of light depends on its variation, the oscillation between its presence and its absence. Alongside Merleau-Ponty we must ask, "Why not admit what Proust knew very well and said in another place—that language as well as music can sustain a sense by virtue of its own arrangement, catch a meaning in its own mesh."[10] Weaving dark and light, day-lighting interiors is a bare minimum. We can sculpt with shadows using textures, folds, and undulations. Warped and overlapped forms and surfaces, pattern, light, sound, and heat move rhythmically in troughs and crests. More immune to temperature fluctuations, a wall that undulates will also resonate in a more complex arrangement of sound and echo.

Rhythm is a function of culture. Edward T. Hall writes, "Human beings are capable of learning to synchronize with any human rhythm provided they start early enough."[11] Human rhythms occur in a broad spectrum ranging from a single moment to the enduring rhythms that chart the rise and fall of civilizations over centuries. Steen Eiler Rasmussen pointed out that the Spanish Steps in Rome are the "petrification of the dancing rhythm of a period of gallantry [that give us] an inkling of something that was, something our generation will never know."[12] Just as the Spanish Steps concretized the rhythmic gestures of the Baroque waltz, our monoscape was patterned by the tonal flat line introduced by the machines of the Industrial Revolution. "The flat line in sound emerges as a result of an increased desire for speed. Rhythmic impulse plus speed equals pitch. Whenever impulses are speeded up beyond twenty occurrences or cycles per second, they are fused together and are perceived as a continuous contour. Increased efficiency in manufacturing, transportation and communication systems fused this older sound into new sound energies of flat line pitched noise," observes Schafer, who

P_ Wall, Andrew Kudless

further warns that the flat line produced by the machine became a "narcotic to the brain and listlessness increased in modern life."[13]

The flat line is self-perpetuating. Uninterrupted smooth surfaces and big box spaces depend on the auxiliary support of more humming machines: forced-air heating and cooling, piped-in muzak, and theme lighting. Thoughtful material selection, careful experimentation, appropriate scale, integral thermal features are all factors essential to the design of human habitat. Thorough study of these variables takes time, an endangered "commodity" in the modern world. In order to design a habitat fit for humans, first we need to slow down. Pauses not only allow for invention, a carefully conceived project can create heirloom solutions.

Because the rhythmic tempo of contemporary culture is moving faster, we have less time to adjust to the changes that are already occurring. The feedback loop keeps tightening, yet healthy buildings like healthy organisms can only grow in a regulated, phased manner. It is unregulated, out-of-phase growth that characterizes cancer. In its unhinged growth, the cancer cell consumes and eventually destroys its environment.

William Condon, who initiated the study of human rhythms said, "There is a genuine coherence in the things we perceive and think about and the coherence is not something we create, but something we discover . . . The temporal is basic and involves history. Processes have their histories. There are many histories, so that while history is pluralistic, it is not therefore discontinuous."[14] Praising the interesting overlaps of history contrasts our deeply ingrained idea of eternity as a static condition to be achieved once we have finally conquered the limits of time. Cyclic rhythms define life. It is arrogant to pretend that our architecture is timeless, somehow standing outside the rigors of time. Perhaps we should seek a *perennial* architecture, one that is renewed by the seasons and the cycles of light and refreshed in the enactment of human ritual. The historian John Ruskin said, "Imperfection is in some sort essential to all that we know of life. It is the sign of life in a mortal body, that is to say, a state of process and change. Nothing that lives is or can be rigidly perfect; part of it is decaying, part nascent . . . and in all things that live, there are certain irregularities and deficiencies, which are not only signs of life, but signs of beauty."[15]

This successive fluctuation between opposites, in which one state flows into the next, is continuum not container. Like the moon's light, its beauty is both fragile and enduring. But dazed by the drone of the flat line, ours is a world where only the Extreme gets registered. The oracular Nietzche wrote, "slack and sleeping senses must be addressed with roaring thunder, but beauty speaks softly only to the most awakened souls." Nuance is absent from the contemporary architecture that narcissistically mirrors our quest for eternal youth through technological means. When we bulldoze habitats or chainsaw trees that predate the birth of Christ just as we iron out our wrinkles with the swift cut of a scalpel, we can expect time to seek its revenge. We have forgotten Ovid's words: "Earth and all her creatures change, and we, as part of creation also must suffer change."[16]

Unable to accept senescence and decay, our buildings reify the frozen idealization of Platonic form and absolute time. Pallasmaa observes, "Instead of offering positive qualities of vintage and authority, time and use attack our buildings destructively."[17] Why not work *with* these inevitable forces rather than fighting *against* them? In their book, *On Weathering*, Mohsen Mostafavi and David Leatherbarrow question whether the process of weathering must always be a subtractive process. Cannot weathering also enhance? Meister Eckhart said, "The soul grows by subtraction not by addition."[18] We can ensoul a building through sensitive, thoughtful use of materials and detailing that celebrate the exigencies of evolutionary time.

For instance, the changes wrought by the natural processes of patinization and oxidation speak the language of elemental alchemy. The interchange between materials and their environment that occurs in oxidation is a living process that records the interaction of one element with another to create a third. Natural materials essentially express the passage of time. The rings of trees expand or contract with the elemental characteristics of the season. The girth of the bountiful rain season is traced concentrically beside the arid stretches of subsequent years. Each grain in the wood embodies memory. Wind and weather expose and clarify its grain patterns. Like hair, resinous woods soften from blond and red to silver and platinum. Materials expose the rigors of time just as your face does. Each crease wears a story, traces a grimace, and records every laugh.

The Japanese cherish the way in which use creates luster. As Tanizaki writes, "We do not dislike everything that shines, but we do prefer a pensive luster to a shallow brilliance, a murky light, whether in stone or artifact, bespeaks a sheen of antiquity . . . Of course this 'sheen of antiquity' of which we hear so much is in fact a glow of grime. In both Chinese and Japanese the words denoting this glow describe a polish that comes of being touched over and over again, a sheen produced by the oils that naturally permeate an object over long years of handling—which is to say grime. If indeed, 'elegance is frigid,' it can as well be described as filthy . . . Westerners attempt to expose every speck of grime and eradicate it, while we Orientals carefully preserve and even idealize it. Yet for better or for worse we do love the things that bear marks of grime, soot and weather, and we love the colors and the sheen that call to mind the past that made them. Living in these old houses among these old objects is in some mysterious way a source of peace and repose."[19]

When visiting the Japanese temples in Nikko one admires the way the grains of wood on the steps in front of the temple are worn smooth by generations of stocking-covered feet. The daily removal of shoes in preparation for prayer burnishes the wood. Cobblestones trafficked by generations of walkers have a similar effect. When polished like this, a glossy film develops on the outer surface, which permits the light to shine through until it is arrested by the rough layer below it. This multi-dimensional effect is produced from seeing the inner layer and the outer layer simultaneously, a shimmering not unlike sunlight tossed about on the surface of water. Glass and metal, no matter how much they are polished, will not yield this effect of depth.

It can take generations to create depth. Chartres, like many of the great cathedrals, is a concentration of more than a dozen building campaigns and one-and-a-half centuries of unrelenting passion. Victor Hugo wrote:

> Great buildings, like great mountains are the work of ages. Often art undergoes a transformation while they are pending completion . . . a shoot is grafted on, the sap circulates, a fresh vegetation burgeons. Truly there is matter for mighty volumes; often indeed for a universal history of mankind, in these successive layers of different periods of art on different levels of the same edifice. The artist, the man, the individual are lost sight of on these massive piles that bear no regard for authorship; they are a summation and totalization of human intelligence. Time is the architect—a nation, the builder.[20]

Time cannot be considered apart from place. The sculptor Andy Goldsworthy noticed, "Real change is best understood by staying in one place. When I travel, I see differences rather than change . . . I thrive on the disruption forced by seasonal changes—a hard freeze, a heavy snow, a sudden thaw, leaf fall, strong winds."[21] The ephemeral passage of seasons underlies the authority of Goldsworthy's work. Similarly, Micheal Van Valkenburgh's *Krakow Ice Garden* mutates seasonally. In spring, purple clematis adorn the steel mesh structure, followed by morning glories in summer, and crimson ivy in the fall. By way of drip irrigation, the wall crystallizes to ice during the winter. The succession of material, living color is reminiscent of Linneaus' flower clock. Water's seasonal phase change powerfully portrays natural transformation.

Michael Van Valkenburgh, Krakow Ice Garden

Krakow Ice Garden (detail)

When discussing the variations of cracking in his installations of clay floor and walls, Goldworthy says, "I can feel the presence of those who have gone before me. This puts my own life into context. My touch is the most recent layer of many layers that are embedded in the landscape which in turn will be covered by future layers hidden but always present."[22] These works express the fragility and inevitability of the compromises forced upon us by nature. In the New Museum of Contemporary Art in New York, the architects Kazuyo Sejima and Ryue Nishizawa of SANAA, recipients of the 2010 Pritzker Prize, intentionally left out the expansion joints in the polished concrete floor in order to liberate the concrete to move and crack with pressure from feet and thermal and structural forces. A map of motion captured in fissures, this gesture expresses Merleau Ponty's observation that "Every human enterprise is a crystallization of time."[23]

Perhaps nowhere is the deep, rhythmic accretion over time more pronounced than in stone. The history of the earth is written in stone. Strata reveal an immense span of time, billions of years in which ordinary days overlap the cataclysmic inversions and civilization's buried past. Patterns are layered in sediment, ripple marks and flumes witness discontinuities. The geologist James Hutton said that the deep time of geologic history bears "no vestige of a beginning—no prospect of an end." Volumes of events lie dormant within the earth's crust. Scientists can deduce weather patterns from deposits of trace elements. They can map changes in the earth's magnetic field and reversals of polarity over millions of years. When we build, we intervene in this ancient fold. Louis Sullivan wrote of this exceptional responsibility: "The materials of a building are but the elements of earth removed from the matrix of nature, and reshaped and reorganized by force, mechanical, muscular, mental, emotional, moral, spiritual. If these elements are to be robbed of their divinity, let them become fully human."[24]

Once removed from this matrix, various means are available for enhancing or highlighting different aspects of the stone's character. Flaming and chiseling reveal the understory of the material. Honing softens and evens out gradations. Polishing reflects light away from the surface. Carefully executed, these techniques craft new chapters of the life into stone. At the Vietnam War Memorial, Maya Lin used polished granite as a mirror. On the reflection of your face, you see the names of the deceased etched into the stone. Because the names are etched, the letters form depressions in the stone. When you touch the surface, your finger senses the absence of substance. The letters of the departed are literally empty spaces in the solid stone. Such poetic sensibility renders humanity into the hardest of materials.

The plastic quality of concrete and plaster remember the skin of their mold, a palimpsest of memory. Texture and relief invite life. In an exhibit entitled *Sensate* at the San Francisco Museum of Modern Art, the artist and architect Andrew Kudless was surprised to discover that people could not keep their hands off of his bulbous "P_Wall". When the installation was returned to his studio at the completion of the exhibit he found moss growing on it and animals nesting in it.[25]

We all tend to gravitate toward the comfort of the sheltered fold. Heidegger fondly describes a farmhouse in Germany's Black Forest that was sited in the sheltered crease between verdant hills. "The simple oneness of things ordered the house . . . it did not forget the altar corner behind the community table . . . which allowed death and life to coexist . . . It made room in its chamber for the hallowed

Andrew Kudless, Weathered P_Wall

places of the childbed and the tree of the dead, for that is what they call a coffin there."[26] The home was designed for different generations under one roof to each experience the unique character of their perennial journey through time. These are the threads of history and continuity that stabilize life. The future is always shaped by the past. The bulldozer mentality cannot comprehend the complex, fragile, and unrelenting reality that time is a continuum. Every cell

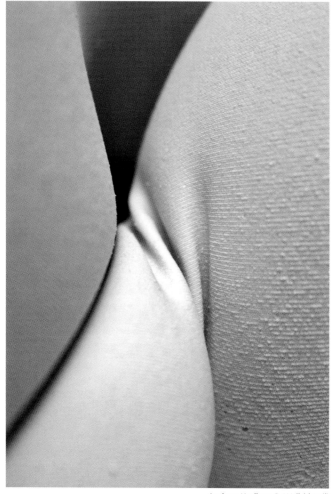

Andrew Kudless, P_Wall (detail)

in our body is composed of the stuff of ancient galaxies, every brick in our city teems with a host of molecules once rimmed in fire. Today's events happen to be the most conspicuous sections of the continuum—like the visible light situated between ultraviolet and infrared wavelengths in the electromagnetic spectrum. Our personal histories are embedded in the vast histories of earth and cosmos. Where do we begin? What if there is no such thing as an end? Mary Oliver wonders, "How could anyone believe that anything in this world is only what it appears to be, that anything is ever final, that anything, in spite of its absence, ever dies a perfect death?"[27]

Hestia enraged

RITUAL: A CIPHER OF TIME

Time does not consecrate that in which she has been ignored.

– French Proverb

Examining the motives that gave rise to the original dwellings in the first chapter of his second book, Vitruvius writes:

> The men of old were born like the wild beasts in woods, caves, and groves and lived on savage fare. As time went on, the thickly crowded trees in a certain place tossed by storms and winds, and rubbing their branches against one another, caught fire, and so the inhabitants of the place were put to flight, being terrified of the furious flames. After it subsided, they drew near, and observing that they were comfortable standing before a warm fire, they put logs on and while keeping it alive, brought other people to it, showing them by signs how much comfort they got from it . . . Therefore it was the discovery of fire that originally gave rise to the coming together of men, to deliberative assembly, and to social intercourse . . . They began in that first assembly to construct shelters. Some made them of green boughs, others dug caves on mountainsides, and some, in imitation of the nests of swallows and the way they built, made places of refuge out of mud and twigs.[1]

According to this account, human dwelling closely followed the discovery of fire. Bringing down the sun propelled the course of human evolution. Fire sparked human invention: the growth of technology, the forging of metals, the development of our extensions, and even the evolution of our bodily form. This Vitruvian legend reveals how intimately the rituals of gathering and dwelling are linked in origin and practice. Fire was brought into every home and sustained within the hearth. For the ancient Greeks, the hearth was the center of every home, the dwelling place of the fire goddess. "The simplest hearth encloses a universe," writes Bachelard.[2] Hestia, the Greek goddess of the hearth, personifies that universe. Even a brief study of her significance in Greek mythology enriches our understanding of what it means to dwell. She personally invites us to enter into the secrets of matter.

Hestia was the firstborn child of Rhea and Kronos and the eldest sister of Zeus. Considered to be both first and last, she was the first to be swallowed by Kronos, and the last to be disgorged. Homer praised her in his *Hymn to Hestia*: "In the high dwellings of all, both deathless gods and men who walk the earth, you have gained an everlasting abode and highest honor: glorious is your portion and your right. For without you, mortals hold no banquet, where one does not duly pour sweet wine to Hestia both first and last." Dedicating an offering to Hestia initiated and concluded every ritual. Her presence was profoundly pervasive, woven as it was into the details of daily life. Unlike other deities in the Greek pantheon, there was no need to dedicate a special temple to her; her relative absence from representation alludes to her sheer necessity and power. As long as her flames were tended, Hestia consecrated each home and transformed it into a sanctuary.

Considered to be the goddess of hospitality, Hestia welcomed all and turned none away. She presided at the communal hearth in the *pyrtaneion*, whose flame was said to be originally taken from the pure light of the sun. A meeting place for citizens and dignitaries, the *pyrtaneion* was the heart of public life in ancient and classical Greece that provided nourishment in the form of ritual banquets. Community decisions made there were sanctioned with Hestia's blessings. As the empire expanded, Hestia's original flame was carried from the communal altar to each new colony. Honoring the symbolic private and public hearth ensured the integrity of each family, on whose healthly functioning the entire community depended. Nurturing Hestia's flame was a strategic necessity critical to sustaining the intricate balance of the entire community.

According to Euripides, "The sages call the Earth-Mother Hestia because she remains motionless at the center." Hestia's presence was embodied in her replica, the sole object that was found in the temple of Delphi. Her body signified the *omphalos*, which protruded from the center of the temple and reached down inside the earth like an umbilicus. The poets and philosophers of the time elaborate on this connection. Philolaus wrote, "The One who is at the center of the Sphere, is the hearth." Ovid confirms, "Vesta [Roman *Hestia*] is the same as the earth." Hestia's warmth was indeed the abiding fire that burns at the center of the earth. The French scholar, Jean Joseph Goux, ties the etymological origins of the Greek word *estia*, from which Hestia derives, to the verb "to be", a root shared by the words essence, substance, and dwelling. In fact, the words earth, heart, and hearth all share etymological core meanings.[3]

Linguistic evidence reinforces the place of the hearth as center, it was the focal point which rooted the dwelling to the forces of the earth. This site of ritual was "*the* passageway par excellence between normally separate and isolated cosmic levels," affirms Jean Pierre Vernant.[4] Hestia attended this inner threshold between worlds; hers was the umbilicus through which powerful silent communication transpired. The Greeks were obsessed with thresholds, and the hearth delineated the most intimate and universal of all thresholds in the dwelling place.

When enacted at the threshold, ritual is, as Alberto Pérez-Gómez says, "a poetic vision realized in space/time."[5] One of the very complex functions of ritual is to unite our most primal urges with our highest aspirations. Vernant suggests, "Another image evoked by the hearth is that of a mast of a ship firmly stepped in the deck and raised straight up towards the sky."[6] Here the hearth, as the liminal space of ritual, is the catalyzing thread stretched between being and becoming. These lines from Rilke's *Sonnets to Orpheus* speak of this tenuous condition:

> Want change, be inspired by the flame
> Where everything is alight as it disappears.
> The artist, when sketching, loves nothing so much
> As the curve of the body turning away.
>
> What locks itself in sameness has congealed.
> Is it safer to be gray and numb?
> What turns hard becomes rigid
> And is easily shattered.[7]

When enacted consciously, ritual sanctifies and transcends mere routine. The practice of ritual effectively transmits knowledge across time because it is patterned and alliterative. Such repetition, to extend Vernant's metaphor, anchors our winged sail to a sturdy vessel and binds together the psychic, social, natural, and cultural orders that the exigencies of life tear apart. Mindful ritual like the orifice of a window framing an expansive view, is a material space of possibility that opens within a body of continuity.

A most dedicated student of the mysteries of matter, Bachelard reminds us that "Reverie sacralizes its object."[8] In *Psychoanalysis of Fire*, he calls fire "the first object of reverie, the symbol of repose, the invitation for repose . . . to be deprived of a reverie before a burning fire is to lose the first and truly human use of fire."[9] The mind of reverie works on multiple dimensions that radiate from the deeply personal outward to the social and cultural. Fire induces reverie in the way that ritual does, which is perhaps why Bachelard considers fire to be "more of a social reality than a natural reality."[10]

Evidence suggests that our remote ancestors were ritualizing before they became human.[11] The practice of ritual engraved our pathway to the human condition. Rooted in the very nature of our embodiment, ritual is an experimental way of moving from the inchoate to the expressive, from the pragmatic to the symbolic. In this sense, ritual is the very source of speech, the arts, religion, culture, and ethics. We simultaneously invented rituals and the rituals in turn invented us. The crackling, dancing, and fragrant flames of fire, evoke a state of silent communion, the ground from which all expressions of meaningful communication emerge.

The Vitruvian image of glowing faces and bodies illuminated by flames inspired the original human dwellings. It is not surprising then that the Greeks considered Hestia to be the original architect and builder, a condition that underlies Heidegger's admonition that dwelling is the essential precursor to building. The act of dwelling, he said, is a sort of sparing, a protected space. Hestia symbolizes the centrality of the hearth as the very epitome of ritual space. Our exploration of her importance reveals the intrinsic bond between consciousness and built form. Architecture, in its alliteration of ritual space, shelters the essentially generative impulse that is the ground of discourse. And, like a great hearth, architecture defends the sacralizing flames of daily life.

Yet the remote halcyon image of ancient man gathered before a fire, hardly seems relevant to our modern technological existence. The hearth in most homes has gone cold. The dancing flames that once animated the center of every home have been replaced with the flicker of the television. The way many people see fire is through a virtual image on a monitor, destitute of aroma, sound, and heat. Yet if this need is so indisputably primary, how is it being expressed today? We need not look farther than our own belly. By illustrating how our digestive system coevolved with fire, primatologist Richard Wrangham proposes a new theory of human origins. In his book, *Catching Fire: How Cooking Made Us Human*, he suggests, "The introduction of cooking may have been the decisive factor in leading our remote ancestors from a primarily animal existence to a more fully human one."[12] Compared to primates we have small mouths, teeth, stomachs, colons, and guts. Cooking gave us an extraordinary evolutionary advantage because cooked food is easier to digest. Since digestion consumes almost as much energy as locomotion, cooking enabled us to gain more energy with less food. Our brain requires an inordinately large amount of energy, approximately twenty percent of our total base metabolic rate. So, increased energy efficiency enabled us to grow uniquely large brains. Cooking not only gave us gorgeous smiles, actual waistlines, and refined taste buds, it gave us exquisitely brilliant minds.

Bachelard relishes telling us that our digestive system is the interiorization of fire: "Fire is an element which is at the center of each living thing."[13] Our belly "is a hearth, in which the indestructible fire principle is smoldering . . . invisible fire, fire without the flame."[14] A true French gastronome, Bachelard exalts the "great and wholly inward certainties of digestion—the pleasant comfort of hot soup, the wholesome warmth of the alcoholic stimulant."[15] His was the first book of philosophy to ever make my mouth water.

Bachelard anticipated the cooking theory of human origins by seven decades. Comparing our digestive system to the element of fire harkens back to Hestia's embodiment of heat at the center of the earth. Similarly, in Hindu cosmology the third chakra is situated at the belly and is associated with the fire element. In the Sumerian empire the site of ritual offerings was the *kitche*. Jung said, "In practical matters, especially in the kitchen where one should really have an open fire, there are to be found mysterious ecstasies of which the purely functionally minded never dream."[16] When conducting a radio interview in the Unite Marseilles, Le Corbusier spoke of the kitchen as the "fire, the hearth, that is to say something ancestral, the eternal key to everything."[17] Indeed, few occasions connect us to the earth and to each other more than the simple meal. It is fair to say that Hestia has now taken up residence at the common table.

The dining table is indisputably one of the great civilizing places of life. Making and sharing a meal is a creative act, a conscious affront to consumable commodity. In a world that appears to avail all, where time is sacrificed for efficiency, the ordinary gathering together to enjoy each other and the fruits of our labor, without haste, stitches together the threads that the demands of life tear apart. "Our growth as conscious awake human beings is marked not so much by grand gestures and visible renunciations as by extending loving attention to the minutest particulars of our lives," wrote Zen master Dogen.[18] The ritual of the common meal activates a patterning force that binds together the social fabric. But in our techno-culture's preference for speed, we have substituted the rituals of the table for those associated with "fast food". We are largely ignorant of the terrible psychic and cultural cost we pay for the mass acceptance of "eating on the run".

The pandemic of childhood obesity can be attributed at least partially, to the decline in rituals of the common table. When deprived of the comforting effects of the table, which include food preparation, quality ingredients, and thoughtful eating and conversation, people tend to overeat. The overwhelming emphasis and reward for filling our time with constant activity at the expense of genuine human contact around a shared table, contributes to a loss of meaning that no amount of food can replenish. Because of fast food and eating on the run, our current generation of children is the first to have a shorter life expectancy than their parents. And for this neglect, on some primal strata of our collective psyche, Hestia weeps.

Cicero proclaimed that "A sick soul was one which could not attain or endure and was always astray." In this statement he has precisely diagnosed our techno-culture. As the French proverb that opened this chapter says, "Time does not consecrate that in which she has been ignored." When not honored, she withdraws, or worse, we suffer her revenge. For the Greeks, Hestia was the heart of every ritual and the recipient of its first blessings. She was "the guardian of the innermost things" who embodied the profound essence of all rituals. The ancient Greeks knew that anchoring her vast energies to the center of every home was crucial to the preservation of civilization. Abraham Maslow reminds us, "The great lesson from the true mystics . . . is that the sacred is in the ordinary, that it is to be found in one's daily life, in one's neighbors, friends and family, in one's backyard, and that travel may be a flight from confronting the sacred— this lesson can be easily lost. To be looking everywhere for miracles is to me a sure sign of ignorance that everything is miraculous."[19] Dwelling consists of a cycle of ordinary acts and humble rituals. When meaningful rituals vanish from our lives and are thoughtlessly replaced with compulsions and addictions, we activate Hestia's wrath. When untended, Hestia's flames rage out of control. Global warming is fueled by the ravenous appetite and dangerous pathologies of the consumer machine. Sustaining meaning in our lives, nurturing our human connections, creating rather than consuming—a life without these countless small acts of grace is one destined to be engulfed in its own flames.

9

SCULPTING PLAY

There are the mud-flowers of dialect
and the immortelles of perfect pitch
and that moment
when the bird sings very close
to the music of what happens.

– Seamus Heaney

One November at dusk on Canada's Hudson Bay, the German photographer Norbert Rosing was filming a pride of huskies, when a one ton polar bear suddenly entered the scene. Since the solid ice prevented the bear from hunting for seals, he had probably not eaten for four months. What transpired in the ensuing moments has been immortalized on YouTube with millions of views. Rather than going for the dog's jugular as one would expect, the hungry bear frolicked with the dogs and after fifteen minutes wound up flat on his back, completely sated. The experience was so gratifying that the bear returned every night for a week, hoping to play with the dogs. The scene reminds me of my twin boys who wrestle with each other like lion cubs, gratuitously and with utter abandon. No goal, no agenda, completely open-ended, effortless and fun, play is older than people and as basic a phenomenon as sleep.

Like the restorative power of sleep, our brains require play for their basic functioning. With the advent of brain imaging technology, scientists can now study the ways our innate tendency to play sculpts our brain. Playfulness correlates with brain size: larger brains require more play. The amount of play is related to the development of the frontal cortex, the seat of cognition, the area of the brain responsible for discrimination, organizing, attention, language processing, and sensing musical rhythm. Research suggests that through simulation and experimental testing, play channels feedback to the brain, encouraging new cognitive connections. A process of discovery, play is an investigative method, a way of knowing that innovates and strengthens flexibility, adaptability, problem solving, and resilience.

The state of mind we call play is absorptive; it is a quality of attention that is focused but not forced. It is with this taut yet relaxed kind of mind that a musician *plays* his instrument, and an athlete *plays* her game. The art of coaxing the melody from a flute or launching a soccer ball on a delicate arc or re-enacting a gesture on stage, all share an ease borne of practice and familiarity. Perhaps this is why play is fun; it unleashes energy, tunes us into a rhythm. Once in a rhythm, play becomes effortless, like breathing. Among the Native Americans of the Haida tribe, the verb "to breathe" is the same as the verb for "making poetry." It is not trivial that the Latin word for "discover" is the exact same word as "invent". In a state of play, judgment is suspended and possibilities disclose themselves. Discover and invent really mean "to come across". Abandoned in a state of play we can come across novel combinations. The essence of our own language suggests that we don't invent *ex nihilo*; instead we create new material and new means of expression through reassembling and reexamining those that already exist.

Play is a method through which we can situate ourselves at the crossing. The place where, Bachelard says, "the original (creative) impulse is directed into various channels."[1] Poets, artists, and sometimes architects, are well aware of this process. Exploratory play was one secret to the success of the Bauhaus. Johannes Itten who devised the *Vorkurs*, the curriculum for first year students, wanted to cleanse the students of their preconceived notions. He said, "Every new student arrives encumbered with a mass of accumulated information which he must abandon before he can achieve perception and knowledge that are really his own."[2] Influenced by Frederick Froebel and John Dewey, Itten sought to suspend logical thinking through exploratory play. Froebel was himself apprenticed to a forester and land surveyor and had ambitions of becoming an architect. Frank Lloyd Wright famously played with Froebel blocks in his crib. Wright later founded Taliesin, whose curriculum is still based on "learning by doing". The apprenticeship approach that both Wright and Itten embraced is a time-honored technique of simulation, a sort of protected play. Before turning to architecture, Peter Zumthor was apprenticed to a cabinetmaker. The son of a craftsman, he "was brought up in surroundings not devoted to buying and consuming but to making things."[3]

The fact that we continually absorb information from the environment makes the context where learning occurs critically important. Edward T. Hall noticed that the textures of surfaces on and within buildings seldom reflect conscious decisions and afford few opportunities to build a "kinesthetic repertoire of spatial experiences."[4] He suggested that early exposure to textural nuance accounts for the notable spatial sensitivity in certain Asian cultures. Not coincidentally, the Japanese have a proverb that counsels "Don't learn it, get used to it." In the realm of play, we can grow accustomed to complex, intricate, subliminal knowledge that otherwise cannot be taught.

William Blake advised that the "true method of knowledge is experiment." Tactile play is one such experimental design method that unveils fresh knowledge. Under Moholy-Nagy and Josef Albers, the Bauhaus *Vorkurs* changed to a sort of 'play-therapy'. In 1928, an architectural student described the course in this way: "What Albers did was to seat us at long tables in the workshop wing of the Bauhaus and confront us with some unlikely materials such as wire mesh, paper, corrugated cardboard, sheet metal, match boxes, newspapers, or what not. We were supposed to do something with these—just *basteln*, or play around with them, to see if we could make something out of them or discover something about them."[5] Steen Eiler Rasmussen reflects on the Bauhaus curriculum: "By recording their impressions of the various materials they worked with, the students gathered a compendium of valuable information for future use. The tactile sense was trained in experiments with textures systematically arranged according to the degree of coarseness. By running their fingers over the materials again and again, the students were finally able to sense a sort of musical scale of textural values."[6]

In today's world, the design firm IDEO has a similar tool with their "tech box," which is at once a materials library, database, website, and a capsule of organizational memory. Each drawer holds hundreds of items from fabrics to toys, each of which is tagged and numbered. The tech box is an invaluable resource that helps designers and engineers gain inspiration, bust out of a rut, or avoid having to reinvent the wheel. Tactility and manipulative object play prove to be critical to our brain's development. The neurologist Frank Wilson has devoted his entire career to studying the interdependent relationship between the brain and the hand. In his view, the brain and hand have co-evolved with each other; the hand provides the means for interacting with the world, while the brain provides the method. He says, "A hand is always in search of a brain and a brain is in search of a hand."[7] Using our hands to play with objects lights up cognition and helps our brain develop beyond strictly manipulative skills.

"The craft of the hand is richer than we commonly imagine . . . All of the work of the hand is rooted in thinking," wrote Heidegger.[8] Drawing with our hands is an essential practice for architects. Our pencil, like Bachelard's "pen who dreams" or the baton in the hand of a symphony conductor, conveys the substance of our imagination. Both Le Corbusier and Aalto sketched incessantly. Le Corbusier practiced a daily discipline of physical exercise, sketching, and painting each morning before heading to his atelier. This rigor effectively opened a space in which he could cultivate his imagination, a scaffolding through which the riches of his unconscious could be accessed. He wrote, "If the generations to come attach any importance to my work as an architect, it is to these unknown labors that one has to attribute its deeper meaning."[9] Inevitably architectural concepts emerged from his unknown labors, but sketching was first a structure of open play, absent of striving.

Mumford pointed out that the "nascent idea, well before it can find words to express itself, first does so in the language of the body."[10] Inherently open-ended, sketching is a tentative process in which ideas can take form over time. Aalto thought with his hands. He said that his solution for the Viipuri library appeared gradually "with the help of primitive sketches from some kind of fantastic mountain landscape."[11] Steven Holl also spends every morning at home sketching and playing with watercolors before he arrives to his New York office. This discipline of play primes receptivity to our instinctual resources. Loren Eisley wrote,

> What seems to characterize the creative person . . . is a relative absence of repression or suppression as the mechanism for the con-

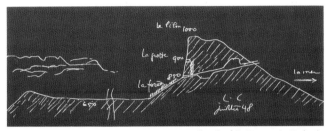

Sketch of St. Baume, Le Corbusier

trol of impulse and imagery. Repression operates against creativity, regardless of how intelligent a person may be, because it never makes available to the person, large aspects of his own experience . . . dissociated items of experience cannot combine with one another; there are barriers to communication among different systems of experience. The creative person, given to expression, rather than repression or suppression, thus has fuller access to his own experience, both conscious and unconscious. Furthermore, because the unconscious operates more by symbols than by logic, the creative person is more open to complex equivalencies in experience, facility in metaphor, being one specific consequence of the creative person's greater openness to his own depth.[12]

Effective problem solving in adulthood has been linked with tactile object play in childhood, recall Wright and his Froebel blocks. Time spent building model airplanes and fixing cars may be equally valuable in training engineers to be innovative problem solvers, as getting an advanced degree. Picasso said, "The artist is a receptacle for emotions, regardless of whether they spring from heaven, from earth, from a scrap of paper, from a passing face, or from a spider's web. That is why he must not distinguish between things. *Quartiers de noblesse* do not exist among objects."[13] Exploratory play opens new cognitive avenues and forges new synaptic connections, there is no privilege among potential catalysts.

The Bauhaus mantra "play becomes party—party becomes work—work becomes play", is a circuit which testifies to the robust creativity that blossomed in a ripe setting with motivated practitioners. As I mentioned previously, the origin of the word work derives from the root *ergon*, as do the words organ and orgasm. In the musical sense, playing an otherwise inanimate organ brings it to life, like the blood that pumps through the organ of our heart. If work is the fruit of our labor, it is not unlike an orgasm being the instantaneous fruit of our love-making. The activity of work, our beating heart, the release of love are all an exercise of an evolutionary impulse. If creativity fundamentally brings new forms to life, play is its implicit *modus operandi*. The erotic undertones of play are evident in many human languages. The Sanskrit word for lovemaking is *kridaratnam*, whose literal translation is "the jewel of games". *Spielkind*, the German word for 'play child', means a child born out of wedlock.

R.W. Gerard made an analogy between the human creative process and biological evolution back in 1946 when he suggested that imagination is to ideas what mutation is to animals. Both processes create a diversity of new forms more or less viable and well-suited to the requirements of their environment than those that already exist. Though some of the forms may possess only several new features, they may prove to be precisely the ones that are not only adaptive, but novel. The imagination, accessed through play, opens evolutionary pathways. Darwin wrote in his autobiography:

> Poetry of many kinds . . . gave me great pleasure, and even as a schoolboy I took intense delight in Shakespeare, especially in the historical plays. I have also said that formerly pictures

gave me considerable, and music very great delight. But now for many years I cannot endure to read a line of poetry; I have tried lately to read Shakespeare, and found it so intolerably dull it nauseated me. I have also lost any taste for pictures or music ... My mind seems to have become a kind of machine for grinding general laws out of large collections of fact, but why this should have caused atrophy of that part of the brain alone, on which the higher tastes depend, I cannot conceive ... The loss of these tastes is a loss of happiness, and may possibly be injurious to the intellect, and more probably to the moral character, by enfeebling the emotional part of our nature.[14]

Darwin's successors unfairly reduced his theory of natural selection to the survival of the fittest, when in fact evolution advances through a complex web of relations rather than through competition alone. Unforced, play provides the setting for complex relationships to sort and puzzle themselves out. The alchemists did not add or subtract chemicals to and from each other to invent a new substance. They did not follow a cookbook full of recipes. Transformation of substance was effected through a change of relationship. But, unfortunately, the situation hasn't changed much since the turn of the last century when Louis Sullivan lamented that the young architect, "has been told that architecture is a fixed, a real, a definite, a specific thing, that all is done and arranged ... He is allowed to believe that when his turn comes ... he can dip it out of his books with the same facility that a grocer dipping beans out of a bin. He is taught by the logic of events that architecture in practice is a commercial article, like a patent medicine, unknown in its mixture and sold exclusively to the public on Brand."[15] This stems from the fact that "Everything literal, formal, and smart in his nature has been encouraged—the early and plastic glow to emotion and sensibility has been ignored."[16] Play is a method of learning that cultivates the early plastic glow we all have buried beneath our clothing of smartness. It avails knowledge that is visceral and intuitive of the sort that Homer believed to be the seat of human identity and intelligence. The aesthetic experience that Borges describes as a "physical sensation, something we feel with our whole bodies. It is not the result of a judgment. We do not arrive at it by way of rules. We either feel it or we don't."[17] The Japanese have the concept of *kufu*, which D.T. Suzuki describes as,

> Not just thinking with the head, but the state when the whole body is involved in and applied to the solving of a problem . . . It is the intellect that raises a question, but it is not the intellect that answers it . . . The Japanese often talk about 'asking the abdomen' or 'thinking with the abdomen', or 'seeing or hearing with the abdomen'. The abdomen which includes the whole system of viscera, symbolizes the totality of one's personality . . . Psychologically speaking, [*kufu*] is to bring out what is stored in the unconscious, and let it work itself out quite independently of any kind of interfering consciousness . . . One may say, this is literally groping in the dark, there is nothing quite indicated, we are lost in the maze. [18]

In our complicated global world, interdisciplinary endeavors are not only imperative they are inescapable. Specialized knowledge ultimately makes sense only in relation to broader fields of knowledge. In fact, the rapid advances of cognitive science can be partially attributed to its native interdisciplinarity. The "compartmentalization of occupations and interests brings about separation of that mode of activity commonly called 'practice' from insight, from imagination, from executive doing of significant purpose from work of emotion from thought and doing," John Dewey pointed out.[19] The era of the autocratic architect has gone the way of the executive authority in the brain, both are anachronisms. Creating a building and knitting into the urban fabric is a complex endeavor requiring many minds and hands.

The evolution of ideas progresses dramatically through interdisciplinary discourse around a common table. In a brainstorming session or a board meeting, the mind becomes communal, no one person has all of the information, nor is any one person in complete control. By listening and thinking out loud, through playing together with open alternatives, we venture into uncharted territories none of us could have visited alone. In abandoning the Cartesian paradigm, we must also abandon the belief that we own our own minds. Our minds are unconscious and conscious; material and immaterial, subjective and objective and ultimately as collective as they are individual.

10

LOVE IS PAYING ATTENTION

For a homebody surrounded by the familiar or a traveler
exploring the strange,
there can be no better guide to a place than the weight of its air,
the behavior of its light, the shape of its water,
the textures of rock and feather, leaf and fur
and the ways that humans bless, mark or obliterate them.
Each of us possesses five fundamental enthralling maps to the natural
world: sight, touch, taste, hearing and smell.
As we unravel the threads that bind us to nature,
as denizens of data and artifice,
amid crowds and clutter,
we become miserly with these loyal and exquisite guides,
we numb our sensory intelligence.
This failure of attention will make orphans of us all.

– Ellen Meloy

As the scene opens, we witness the hero smoking a cigarette while talking on the phone, texting with one hand and holding the steering wheel with the other, no sign of a seat belt. While we can quickly deduce that we are watching a French film, this scenario is not all that exaggerated. Next time you are waiting in line, find someone who is actually daydreaming or observing their surroundings; this is an endangered sight. Driving, waiting, sitting around, these occasions for idleness are increasingly filled with busyness and productive multi-tasking. Numerous books and articles in recent years have lamented the disintegration of our attention span and questioned whether "Google is Making Us Stupid".[1] Modern life is driving us to distraction, but so what? The problem is that distraction is a centrifugal force that unravels our capacity for sustained, perceptive attention.

Such an unbinding has serious implications. The single quality that distinguishes geniuses of all kinds, according to William James, is the capacity for sustained voluntary attention. He defined attention as "the taking possession by the mind, in clear, vivid form of one out of what seem several simultaneously possible objects or trains of thought."[2] He thought that attention profoundly influenced character and ethical behavior. Our ability to repeatedly focus a wandering attention lies at the root of judgment, will, and creative potential—the very determinants of cultural progress. B. Alan Wallace, in his book, *Attention Revolution,* wonders, "Might 'genius' be a potential we all share—each of us with a unique capacity for creativity, requiring only the power of sustained attention to unlock it?"[3] Indeed, mental focus permits the creative spark to percolate to the surface of consciousness, whereas distraction prevents us from realizing our creative potential.

We now know that consciousness and our capacity to pay attention is highly amenable to change. Neuroplasticity is inherent in our constitution and scientists daily discover the extent to which the attention can be either developed or eroded. James believed that an education of our attention was an education of the highest sort. Given the malleability and fundamental importance of paying attention, it is remarkable that attention training is virtually nonexistent in our education systems or for that matter anywhere outside a Zendo.

Abundant experimental evidence demonstrates that perceptual skill can be sharpened with training. The key change from the beginning to end of the experiments was the level of attention. Attention can be cultivated. Zen meditation practice is dedicated to such an endeavor: the sharpening of subtlety, refining the mind, allowing not forcing. Through paying attention, we tend to notice critical differences and fewer irrelevancies. "Intelligence is paying attention to the right things," wrote Dewey.[4] Sara Lazar, the Director of the Massachusetts General Hospital Laboratory for Neuroscientific Investigation of Meditation, has found that people who meditate develop denser, thicker networks of neurons in the pre-frontal cortex and right anterior insula of their brains, the areas that govern attention and sensory processing.[5]

If we can be still long enough, details of the world reveal themselves of their own accord. Steven Holl counsels, "To open ourselves to perception, we must transcend the mundane urgency of 'things to do'. We must try to access the inner life which reveals the luminous intensity of the world. Only through solitude can we begin to penetrate the secret world around us. An awareness of one's unique existence in space is essential in developing a consciousness of perception."[6] Rather than forcing our experience into a prefixed Platonic ideal or the totality of a planner's prescription, contextual information is simply allowed to emerge. This is deep listening, the source of both poetic making and responsible action.

Not to be confused with passivity or giving up, this awareness is a participatory acceptance and understanding of the whole situation as it manifests through the details. This state of being permits us to experience the vibrance of specificity. Paying attention allows us to experience the uniqueness and authenticity of the situation itself, not as an echo of our self. In *Thinking Architecture*, Peter Zumthor discusses how his design for the Thermal Baths at Vals did not begin with forms or ideas that were to be adapted to the site, "but by endeavoring to answer basic questions arising from the location of the given site, the purpose and the building materials—mountains, rock, water—which had no visual content in terms of existing architecture. It was only when we succeeded in answering step by step, the questions posed by the site, purpose, and material that structures and spaces emerged which surprised us and which I believe possess the potential of a primordial force that reaches deeper than the mere arrangement of stylistically conceived forms."[7] This is deep listening, a process that does not so much pursue new facts as it simply allows phenomena to disclose themselves.

The vibrance of specificity does not admit the easy solutions of formalism or fame's calculated autograph. Through listening and observing, appropriate form emerges from the unique variables of the situation. Local insight yields diverse outcomes. This is perhaps why much of what indigenous cultures produce bears the signature of their landscape. Being situated is to be at the site, the unique unrepeatable place that is context. Situational architecture is appropriate to the enmeshed contexts of time, use, place, and people. Form evolves from these myriad voices. It is an outgrowth of the complex interplay of variables, the intricacy of relationships, and the function of their boundaries. Evolution does not advance through imposition, but through emergence and relationship. We recognize patterns of emergence through an attitude of allowing that does not deny the rational mind but accepts that it is insufficient to complete the job. Accessing this "primordial force" requires, as Alberto Pérez Gómez recommends, "engaging dimensions of consciousness usually stifled by technical education."[8]

"Each new situation requires a new architecture," is Pritzker prize winning architect Jean Nouvel's mantra. His *Louisiana Manifesto* is a paean to the uniqueness of the individual and the personality of place. Nouvel practices a sort of acupuncture of the situation that taps into the pre-existing genius loci of places. In essence, he penetrates the latent energies that give rise to inimitable, novel forms. Through the quality of his attentive mind, he allows the situation to grow into its own best self. He is himself implicated in the investigation. Scientists have had to come to terms with the fact that observation—in effect, paying attention—changes the experiment. The most scrupulously executed experiment undermines the arrogance of objectivity and demonstrates the inherently participatory nature of observation and intention. The phenomenal object of the experiment entrains rhythmically with subjective attention. Edward T. Hall points out that "It is paradoxical that velocity, which under ordinary circumstances would be unmanageable, appears to slow down and become manageable when the right rhythm is established. In fact, it is a fundamental truth of Zen that straining is the enemy of rhythm. Also, whatever the performance, the more perfect the rhythm, the easier it is for another person to perceive the details of what is taking place before his eyes."[9] The clarity of the details emerge when a rhythm has been established, the rhythm inherent in love.

Love is paying attention. Love, strictly relegated to private and dismissed in public discourse, underlies all truly generative work. Alberto Pérez-Gómez warns, "A partial or total ignorance of the deep relationship between love and architectural meaning has dire consequences, perpetuating the modern epidemic of empty formalism and banal functionalism, condemning architecture to passing fashion or consumable commodity, and destining the cultures it frames to their present dangerous pathologies."[10] He suggests, rather, an architecture "built upon love [that] engages the inhabitant as true participant, unlike the remote spectator of the modernist work of art or the consumer of fashionable buildings-cum-images."[11] After many years of teaching, Edward T. Hall noticed that if he couldn't love his students, the class never went well. The rhythm of the class would constantly change and refused to settle down. He said, "Somehow the idea must be accepted that the greatest pleasure and real expression of love on the part of the teacher is to be able to watch and occasionally encourage the talent of each member of the group to grow ... This means that we strive to bring out the best in each other and to somehow allow the rhythm of the group to establish itself and to avoid at all costs the imposition of the artificial rhythm of a fixed agenda."[12] He identified a strong relationship between rhythm and love. He said, "Rhythm and love may be viewed as part of the same process. People in general don't sync well with those they don't like and they do with those they love. Both love and rhythm have so many dimensions that the rhythmic relationship to love might be easily misinterpreted."[13]

The Zen master Uchiyama complained that the prefabricated houses cropping up everywhere in Japan look fine for a couple of years, "but then they begin to look like chicken coops. The realtors who build them are thinking only of their own profit. They have no trace of feeling for viewing their work as a parent sees a child."[14] Over the years, I have also noticed that if I am in sync with my clients, the project goes well. Sometimes this happens instantaneously, at other times our communication grows more fluid over time. In either case, the capacity to listen to what is not being said, to look for signs of what lifted the voice, to listen better to the wind—this attitude enhances the potential for quality work and lasting relationships.

The cognitive scientists tell us that it takes time for the conscious mind to extract latent patterns within a diversity of superficially different experiences. In our idle moments, in the gaps between our activities our minds are busy connecting the threads of our experiences. Idleness can allow epistemic openings, where apparently separate notions mingle and recombine in surprising ways. If these gaps are plugged up by more data, creative synthesis is blocked. The plastic inquiring mind that is receptive and attentive is a quality we inherited from our animal ancestors. But of course, in our cultural emphasis on speed and efficiency this slower mode of consciousness is considered highly suspect. Shoji Hamada, a master potter who is considered to be a living treasure in Japan, confessed that he did not feel authentic or mature until well into his seventies. In speaking about some of his work of which he was particularly proud, he said it did not come from "my mind, it came but from my whole body; it emerged out of my middle, my lower abdomen. I have such a good feeling about having done this pot . . . This work does not come out of my thought; rather I simply permit the movement that my hands have learned over many years. In fact, in the work forged by my body during sixty years, there is an unconscious revelation. I sense that my work has become more comfortable . . . I now hope that, rather than made things, born things will increase in my work."[15] Similarly, Merleau-Ponty praised Paul Klee's colors to have been born upon the canvas, they were naturally exhaled at the right place.

The Japanese believe that your *hara*, their term for the core of your being, lives about two inches above and one inch in from your navel. The attentive mind is not circumscribed in the compass of our skulls, it is closer to our belly button. For Vitruvius too, "The navel is naturally the exact center of the body. For if man lies on his back with hands and feet outspread, and the center of a circle is placed on his navel, his fingers and toes will be touched by the circumference."[16] Sitting upright, breathing through your center is the essential practice of Zen. When we sit still long enough, we begin to discern patterns in the rhythms that surround us. "Design is not making beauty. Beauty emerges from selection, affinities, integration, and love," said Louis Kahn.[17] The process of emergence takes time and the full engagement of our patient, attentive mind. If we fail to cultivate these nascent abilities, we risk becoming a society of mere decoders of information and followers of form, whose false sense of knowing distracts us from deeper cultivation of our creative potential. When Annie Dillard was asked by *Life* magazine, "What is the meaning of life?" she replied simply, "Pay attention so that creation need not play to an empty house."[18]

Taliesin West

11

–––

BELONGING

It was odd, she thought, how if one was alone,
one leant to inanimate things; trees, streams, flowers;
felt they expressed one; felt they became one;
felt they knew one,
in a sense were one.

– Virginia Woolf

Paul Valery gave us a hint when he said the secret of the blackness of milk is accessed through its whiteness. So, when thinking about place, let's first consider its other side, the notion of *replacement*. To replace means to put something back together again. Modernity is full of occasions to re-place. Our sophisticated medicine enables us to replace worn out parts of our body. The hallmark of a well-run company is to make any one of its employees, regardless of how uniquely gifted they may be, replaceable. We tear down communities, to replace them with 'better' ones. Most often, it is cheaper to replace something, than it is to repair it. The ability to replace means that we must first isolate and then remove, to successfully replace anything, means that it must be a component part, of something else. Replace-ability is founded upon reductionism, the practice of reducing wholes down to their component parts. A reductivist approach works wonderfully for mechanics, physics, and certain wine-based sauces. But we have finally realized that reductionism does not work when applied to living systems. Organisms are the sum of thousands of physiological processes that function in concert with one another. By their very nature, they possess no fundamental unit or central aspect that is more basic than any other. How do we then replace a 'part' if its integrity depends on the whole?

Perhaps replacement is impossible for living systems. If we accept that the removal of one part does affect the whole, for better or worse, we would be less cavalier about jettisoning centuries of growth. A most devastating modern menace is the loss of meaning which stems from the sense that we are dispensable parts of a mechanism. Our environment mirrors what we have come to believe about our relations and ourselves: that all are re-*place*-able, the palpable echo of Cartesian solopcism. The natural environment, local culture, and social patterns, once dominant factors shaping the character of a place, are now only marginal determinants. Presently, global economic criteria driven by consumer market forces primarily determine where people live. Dislocated from the tissue of community, people are routinely forced to start *tabula rasa*, a norm all the more insidious because it is equated with freedom.

The banality of the monoscape is one consequence of considering places primarily in terms of economic utility and expedience. Yet in the not so distant past, people were commonly named after places: St. Francis of Asissi, Eleanor of Aquitaine, Leonardo DaVinci, to name a few. Places were not commodities, they were dense contexts of communally-lived history as well as a source of one's personal identity. When he first visited San Diego, my husband, Paolo, who grew up in a village in Italy, was shocked to discover that the streets were "named" after numbers and letters of the alphabet. This erasure of personality, like Alberti's grid, mistakes the surveyor's map for the place itself.

When Merleau-Ponty said, "There is a mythical space in which directions and positions are determined by residence in it of great affective entities," he was describing the lived space that is *place*. Such locations pattern our memories, feelings, images, meanings, and the workings of the imagination.[1] Our feelings about a particular place may be personal, but the feelings grow out of collective experiences that do not occur elsewhere. They are specific to and belong to the place. People and place participate in one another's sustenance, and places perish along with the disappearance of people who cherish them. We dwell in places in a paradigm of mutual influence. Arnold Berleant writes, "There is a reciprocity, an intimate engagement with the conditions of life, that joins person with place in a bond that is not only mutually complementary but genuinely unified."[2] Similarly, E.V. Walter calls place, "a location of mutual immanence, a unity of affective presences abiding together."[3]

Belonging, in the abiding sense of being at home in the world, was commonplace for the ancient Greeks. They shared with other primeval cultures the experience of an animate world in which every corner was inhabited by gods. Plato wrote *Timaeus* when Greece was on the cusp of the old mythic worldview, before the new rationalist intellectual order took hold. *Timaeus* bridges these two ways of thinking; its arguments address the intellect while the images painted with words provoke poetic associations. In this work, Plato uses two different words to describe a place: *topos* was used to describe the physical characteristics of a place and was eventually adopted by Aristotle to describe an objective position. It lies at the root of the word *topography*. To describe the expressive, experiential quality of place, Plato used the word *chora*, which had appeared in Hesiod and the Homeric Hymns and is the oldest Greek word for place. Plato understood *chora* to "underlie all of creation, of which fire, earth, water, and air are only qualities." It is the *prima matera*, a receptacle of all "visible and sensible things" that is itself "invisible and formless, all embracing, possessed in a most puzzling way of intelligibility, yet very hard to grasp."[4]

The dream-like, elusive quality of *chora* was so hard to grasp, in fact, that its meaning is absent from modern connotations of place. We inherited the Aristotelian notion of an objective *topos*, a neutral container. *Chora* was forced underground where it finds expression at the root of the words such as choreography and chorus. But Plato's experiential space, *chora,* continues to flourish. It lies at the heart of the vestigial feeling that most of us secretly harbor about certain places. It is the place that surround us, but not as a sealed, objective container. The philosopher Luce Iriguay suggests this metaphor of place: "half-open and partially touching lips, the hard shell of the containing surface becomes the soft sheath of erotic engagement."[5] In other words, place is space, incarnate.

Chora is the "properly human space" that Alberto Pérez-Gómez describes as "the space of human communication that is inherently bounded and ambiguous. Like the substance of our dreams, we may conceive it only indirectly through spurious reasoning. Yet without it, we simply cannot account for reality."[6] *Nothos* is the Greek antonym for reason, it is typically translated as either spurious or bastard. The Greek word *skotie* also means bastard, but was more poetic and literally meant "one who was born in the dark" or "darkling". Spurious reason can be understood to be knowledge that is born in the dark, from the shadowed depths of the unconscious mind. As skin-covered liminal space, *chora* opens an understanding of place that is not passive, but one that interacts dynamically with the consciousness. Considered as an aspect of the unconscious mind, *chora* is the site of pure potentiality, like the dark matter that nurtures form and by nature forbids access to the intellect alone. It cannot be seen directly, only witnessed through the warping effect of gravitational lensing, the dance of light across a blemished stone wall, or through the leap of Basho's frog.

Perhaps we can understand place as a basin of attraction, a matrix that evokes and sustains our imagination. E.V. Walter writes:

> Towns may die for all sorts of reasons, but expressive vitality depends on how a place engages the imagination. A place is dead if the physique does not support the work of the imagination, if the mind cannot engage with the experience located there, or if the local energy fails to evoke ideas, images or feelings . . . "Where do I belong?" is a question addressed to the imagination. To inhabit a place physically but to remain unaware of what it means, or how it feels, is a deprivation more profound than deafness at a concert or blindness in an art gallery. Humans in this condition belong nowhere.[7]

Genuine places are disappearing from our world and the vital places we do have are endangered. One place I personally cherish is Frank Lloyd Wright's Taliesin West, where I lived and studied architecture. The dense experiential field at Taliesin constantly funds my imagination. Originally designed as a desert encampment and balm from frozen Wisconsin winters, Taliesin West was built by dedicated apprentices. Since 1932, Taliesin has continuously educated architects in an atmosphere of protected play and implicit learning.

Taliesin West is inseparable from the primal genius of the land and the usages of the people who inhabit it. It is the very embodiment of Vincent Scully's observation that "Gods and goddesses housed in Greek temples were manifestations of the spirit or 'atmosphere' of the physical surroundings of the temple, a special case of genius loci. The landscape and the temples together form the architectural whole."[8] Taliesin West bears witness to the natural forces of wind, erosion, fire, and time. Truly "built upon love", it is the accretion of generations of sweat, blood, and dedication. Like hundreds of others before and after me, I also participated in building new structures and resuscitating the old. That experience confirmed Victor Hugo's description of the great cathedrals of Europe, that time is the real builder.

While at Taliesin, I lived in a modest shelter—only a veil of canvas walls and a tin roof bound me from the desert. Living among towering saguaro next to the thoroughfare of life that streams through a dry wash taught nature's silent lessons. I felt viscerally the sentiment Rilke captured in his poem, "The artist loves nothing more than the curve of the body, turning away." Deep inside absence lives presence. The desert longs for the water that once covered her. This thirst for water is present everywhere. The flesh of the cactus grows plump or frail according to the amount of water buried inside. One would never judge the antiquity of the Palo Verde trees based on their height since most of their mass is hidden deep underground, in roots that tap the water table. Protecting moisture is the design impetus, capturing breezes and sculpting with shadows. The crenellated skin of the saguaro ebbs and flows seasonally; the folds flatten in winter and deepen in summer cued by water content. The deep folds protect the skin by keeping it in the shade. The buildings do this as they mediate between the land and the people who inhabit them and care for them.

The complex of buildings is functionally connected with choreographed pathways. Even a brief walk is a sensual feast pulsating with rhythm. Stairways with shallow rise and deep treads slow down the gait subtly lifting and lowering one's view, fountains cascade or trickle and pools quietly shimmer, providing fields upon which light can dance and jump. The sweet volatility of the orange grove holds aromas that soften and deepen in unison with the chatter of birds who gather on their branches. Some buildings are half buried, some are topped in complete translucence, all are made with stones from the surrounding desert. Heavy walls with broad bases that taper toward the top are rooted in gravity, while the original canvas roofs appear to take wing above them. Breezes are welcomed through low passageways, or adjusted with flaps and sails. Massive hearths are everywhere, fire crackles at you while you eat or draw.

Taliesin West "produces an aura, a magic, an atmosphere that never ceases to grip those of us who live in it on a daily basis, and even more startling to those who come upon it and experience it for the first time."[9] Generations now have gathered on the grounds, continue to be educated there, celebrate in feasts, play music and drink tea together. It is a place woven together through ordinary ritual and seasonal ceremony. Like an unfolding poem, the meaning of the place is re-enacted again and again by the participants.

Rituals and ceremonies that make and sustain a place are capable of changing our consciousness. Experiencing a sweat lodge ceremony at Taliesin West remains a strong and lasting memory of the binding power inherent in liminal space. In preparation for the ceremony we created a microcosm of the universe. We fashioned the lodge from young willow branches that easily yielded to our touch, and covered the dome with cloth, each remnant a small piece of our lives quilted together to make shelter. We gathered stones and heated them with flames, poured water to release steam. Encircled beneath the dome we were part of all of the elements stitched together. Linda Hogan, a writer from the Chickasaw tribe describes what happens during the ceremony: "We speak. We sing. We swallow water and breathe smoke. By the end of the ceremony it is as if skin contains land and birds. The places within us have become filled. As inside the enclosure of the lodge, the animals and ancestors move into the human body, into skin and blood. The land merges with us. The stones come to dwell inside the person."[10] Such an experience offers a glimpse into a dimension which cannot again be closed.

This experiential knowledge of place is one in which our "body feels the world in feeling itself," as Merleau-Ponty writes.[11] Many places are the incarnate history of civilizations. Some of these places cannot be replaced; perhaps for many it is already too late. But it is not too late to knit back together our net of relations. Places exist because people love and care for them. When we acknowledge the ways we dwell together, we can build in a way that expresses our connections rather than our barriers. E.V. Walter writes,

> I have no quarrel with my colleagues who diagnose urban distress as a problem of planning, or of social justice, or of power, or of economic priorities, or of the restless movement of capital. I think they are correct as far as they go. But I argue that even with power, resources and good intentions, the defective way about thinking about places—the epistemological stumbling block would frustrate most genuine efforts to make or keep a good place. The way in which people think and write about the obvious world ignores the magic of places, the passions of space."[12]

We depend utterly upon meaningful places. Pérez-Gómez writes, "While our reason may be capable of dismissing the quality of the built environment as central to our spiritual well being, our dreams and our actions are always set in some place, and our understanding (of others and ourselves) simply could not be without significant places."[13] The passion for place grows out of and nourishes our sense of belonging in the world. "Earth, isn't this what you want: rising up inside us invisibly once more?" asks Rilke.[14]

Harmony House, Wallace Cunningham

12

TO DWELL IN POSSIBILITY

My body is a field in itself.
– Maurice Merleau-Ponty

*The surface of an organism, it should be remembered, is actually
a boundary between the organism and its environment,
and the boundary is not always or everywhere as clean-cut
as the hairless human philosopher tends to think.*
– James J. Gibson

*Every man is in touch with everything else,
not through his hands though,
but through a bunch of long fibers that shoot out
from the center of his abdomen.
These fibers join a man to his surroundings, they keep his balance.
They give him stability.*
– Carlos Castaneda

"I inhabited a proverb so vast I needed a universe to fill it," wrote a French poet.[1] Their proverb, that humans can do everything except build a bird's nest does indeed hold a universe. Linda Hogan describes the wonder and delight of finding a nest in nature:

> It was in early February, during the mating season of the great horned owls. It was dusk, and I hiked up the back of a mountain to where I'd heard the owls a year before. I wanted to hear them again, the voices so tender, so deep, like a memory of comfort. I was halfway up the trail when I found a soft, round nest. It had fallen from one of the bare-branched trees. It was a delicate nest, woven together of feathers, sage, and strands of wild grass. Holding in my hand in the rosy twilight, I noticed a blue thread was entwined with the other gatherings there. I pulled at the thread a little, and then I recognized it. It was a thread from one of my skirts. It was blue cotton. It was the unmistakable color and shape of a pattern I knew. I liked it, that a thread of my life was in an abandoned nest, one that held eggs and new life. I took the nest home. At home, I held it in the light and looked more closely. There, to my surprise, nestled in the gray green sage, was a gnarl of black hair. It was also unmistakable. It was my daughter's hair, cleaned from a brush and picked up in the sun by a maple tree . . . I didn't know what kind of nest it was, or who lived there. It didn't matter. I thought of the remnants of our lives carried up the hill that way and turned into shelter. That night, resting inside the walls of our home, the world outside weighed heavily against the thin wood of the house. The sloped roof was the only thing between us and the universe. Everything outside of our wooden boundaries seemed so large. Filled with the night's citizens it all came alive . . . the whole world was a nest on its humble tilt, in the maze of the universe, holding us.[2]

Nested in a material embrace, we are held within a rim of possibility. Threads of memory, a fragment of gingham, a strand of hair carried on currents of wind sculpted with pushing breast, our habitat. Every new life is tendered from these labors. The possible is not without limit and no limit is impossible. Galileo's vision of spheres illuminated in perfect clarity has yielded to the enigmatic presence of dark matter, which is everywhere and underlies everything. Our conscious thought grows out of its moist loam. Invisibility is the substrate of the visible. Silence is the other side of sound. Time is more like a river with quiet eddies and swift rapids, than a straight line. The river, though embanked and bound remains free, its flowing waters are always new. And so too our minds, a new dimension once opened, cannot again be closed. When we turn off the lights, hang up our indomitable will and fall into sleep, we drift into an inexplicable consciousness that we share with each other and other creatures. Like Linda Hogan's sensation of the vast expanse beyond her thin enclosure of wooden walls, at night our isolated self fuses: I dream, therefore I am not.

Within an abandoned nest Hogan found fibers of herself. Our dwellings surely are our mirrors. Ours do not reflect relationship. Even though we know that it is relationship that defines life. Rigidly battling the elements, cut off from one another, objects strewn about the landscape, our buildings no longer feel. Perhaps we should think about architecture in the way that Richard Serra considers his sculpture: as an "open and extended field that is precluded when dealing with sculpture as an autonomous object."[3] Continuing to consider architecture as an object is to miss the possible expressions of relationship between ourselves and our world. Imagine instead a field, open and extended, that holds a binding force of potential experience. Field originates in the word *fold*. We are held in folds of earth, twilight, and dawn. Our bodies are full of folds, our brain, our lips, our eyes, the creases and overlaps are there, even if we don't see them. These are the folds that time successively unwraps, a gift of revelation.

A poet has written that the kiss is more important than the lips. Merleau-Ponty said that, "A couple is more real than either of them."[4] It is not that one is more important than the other, it is that the existence of one is utterly dependent upon the other. They do not and cannot exist in isolation. A work of architecture gains its meaning in its kiss, in the experience it elicits in the inhabitant. When we remain outside of the work, it can be nothing more than sterile formalism. After all, we cannot give what we do not ourselves possess. Our experience of place and space shapes our practice and eventually alters the face of the tangible world. We can start from our own rich, attentive, polyphonic experience and approach our work from the questions, how can it engage us, how will this feel against the body, will it tickle, delight, surprise? What sort of light will fall onto skin and retina? Are there places to pause and comfortably rest? How will this sound and taste? What sorts of encounters might occur here? These are questions asked from the deep interiority of our own nerves and tissues.

We have traveled a long distance from the immaculate speck of divinity incarcerated in the body. We no longer have recourse to a transcendent realm of perfect forms. Our best self is not circumscribed in our brain, it dwells in our intimate, empathic, and ecological relationship with *this* world of wood, stone, bone, and skin. Our shapes engrave themselves into our circuitry and can dignify our ordinary and marvelous experience of the world. We can honor our connections with our past, shape our future, and simply grace the cycles of daily life.

NOTES

PREFACE

1.   Karsten Harries, "Building and the Terror of Time," *Perspecta: The Yale Architectural Journal* 19 (1982): 59-69.

2.   Jean-Paul Sartre, *The Emotions: An Outline of a Theory* (1939; New York: Carol Publishing, 1993), 9.

3.   Gaston Bachelard, *Poetics of Space* (1958; Boston: Beacon Press, 1969).

4.   Pierre Teilhard de Chardin, *The Phenomenon of Man* (New York: HarperCollins, 2008).

5.   Bachelard, *Poetics of Space*, 92.

6.   Edward O. Wilson, *Biophilia* (Cambridge, MA and London: Harvard University Press, 1984), 37.

7.   Joseph Brodsky, "An Immodest Proposal," in *On Grief and Reason* (New York: Farrar, Strauss and Giroux, 1997), 207.

8.   Bachelard, *Poetics of Space*, xxxiv.

9.   As quoted in Bachelard, *Poetics of Space*, 137.

10. Maurice Merleau-Ponty, *The Phenomenology of Perception*, trans. Colin Smith (London: Routledge and Kegan Paul, 1962), 407.

11. As quoted in Liisa Enwald, ed., "Lukijalle," in *Rainer Maria Rilke: Hiljainen taiteen sisin; kirjeitä vuosilta 1900-1926* (Helsinki: TAI-teos, 1997), 8.

12. Maurice Merleau-Ponty, "The Intertwining—The Chiasm," *The Visible and the Invisible*, ed. Claude Lefort (Evanston, IL: Northwestern University Press, 1992).

13. George Lakoff and Mark Johnson, *Metaphors We Live By* (Chicago and London: The University of Chicago Press, 1980), 3.

14. Arnold H. Modell, *Imagination and the Meaningful Brain* (Cambridge, MA and London: The MIT Press, 2006), xii.

15. Semir Zeki, *Inner Vision: An Exploration of Art and the Brain* (Oxford: Oxford University Press, 1999), 1-2.

CHAPTER ONE

1. Martin Heidegger, "Building Dwelling Thinking," in *Basic Writings*, ed. and trans. David Farrell Krell (New York: Harper & Row, 1977), 327.

2. Ibid., 332.

3. Friedrich Nietzche, *Untimely Meditations* (Cambridge, UK: Cambridge University Press, 1997), 63.

4. George Lakoff and Mark Johnson, *Philosophy in the Flesh* (New York: Basic Books, 1999), 3.

5. Antonio Damasio, *Descartes' Error* (New York: G. P. Putnam's Sons, 1994), xvi.

6. Lewis Mumford, *The Pentagon of Power* (New York: Harcourt Brace Jovanovich, 1964), 417.

7.   Heidegger, *Basic Writings,* 321.

8.   Ibid., 326.

9.   Gaston Bachelard, *Poetics of Space,* 2nd ed. (Boston: Beacon Press, 1994), 91. (All subsequent references will be to this edition.)

10. Victor Hugo, *Notre-Dame de Paris*, book IV (New York: Thomas Cromwell and Co., 1888), 3.

11. Heidegger, *Basic Writings*, 338.

12. Jules Michelet, *L'Oiseau,* trans. W.H. Davenport Adams, (London: T. Nelson and Sons, 1869), 248-9.

13. Ibid., 249.

14. Juhani Pallasmaa, *The Eyes of the Skin,* 3rd ed. (West Sussex, UK: John Wiley and Sons, 2008), 19.

15. Kent Bloomer and Charles Moore, *Body, Memory, and Architecture* (New Haven, CT: Yale University Press, 1977), 44.

16. Eugene Victor Walter, *Placeways: A Theory of the Human Environment*, (Chapel Hill, NC: University of North Carolina Press, 1988), 14.

17. Juhani Pallasmaa, "Hapticity and Time," *Architectural Review* (May 2000): 78-84.

18. Bachelard, *Poetics of Space*, 101.

19. Ibid., 101.

20. In medical terminology, a *nidus* refers to both the spatial origin of a disease and hairy structures such as nerves.

21. James J. Gibson, *Ecological Approach to Visual Perception* (Boston: Houghton Mifflin, 1979), 9.

22. Fritof Capra, *The Web of Life: A New Scientific Understanding of Living Systems* (New York: Anchor Books, 1996), 28.

23. Maurice Merleau-Ponty, *Phenomenology of Perception*, 11th ed. (London: Routledge Classics, 2008), 293.

24. Capra, *The Web of Life*, 28.

25. Samuel Taylor Coleridge, *On Poesy or Art* (1918), in *Biographia Literaria: The Collected Works of Samuel Taylor Coleridge, Biographical Sketches of My Literary Life & Opinions*, eds. James Engell and W. Jackson Bate (Princeton, NJ: Princeton University Press, 1983), 243.

26. As cited in Paul Devereux, *Re-Visioning the Earth: A Guide to Opening and Healing the Channels Between Mind and Nature* (New York: Fireside, 1996), 22.

CHAPTER TWO

1. As cited in Ashley Montagu, *Touching: The Human Significance of the Skin*, 3rd ed. (New York: Harper & Row, 1986), 3.

2. Maurice Merleau-Ponty, *The Visible and the Invisible,* ed. Claude Lefort, trans. Alphonso Lingi (Evanston, IL: Northwestern University Press, 1968), 174.

3. William Blake, "The Marriage of Heaven and Hell," in David Bindman, *William Blake: The Complete Illuminated Books* (London: Thames and Hudson, 2000), 104.

4. Mumford, *Pentagon of Power,* 51-77.

5. Ibid., 33.

6. Ibid., 81.

7. Ibid., 84.

8. Ibid., 59.

9. Alfred North Whitehead, *Science and the Modern World* (New York: Simon and Schuster, 1997), 147.

10. Damasio, *Descartes' Error*, 252.

11. Candace Pert, *Molecules of Emotion* (New York: Simon and Schuster, 1997), 189.

12. Sigfried Giedion, *Space, Time and Architecture: The Growth of a New Tradition*, 5th ed. (Cambridge, MA: Harvard University Press, 1969), 430.

13. Mumford, *The Pentagon of Power*, 56.

14. As cited in Flora Samuel, *Le Corbusier: Architect and Feminist* (London: Wiley-Academy, 2004), 142.

15. Kenneth Frampton, "Of Christos Papoulias," in Catherine David and Kenneth Frampton, *Hypertopos: Two Architectural Projects* (Ostfildern, Germany: Cantz Verlag, 1998), 57.

16. Pallasmaa, *The Eyes of the Skin,* 39.

17. Damasio, *Descartes' Error,* 111.

18. Edward T. Hall, *The Hidden Dimension*, 2nd ed. (New York: Anchor Books, 1990), 4.

19. Andy Clark, *Being There: Putting Brain, Body, and World Together Again* (Cambridge, MA: Bradford/MIT Press, 1997), 217-21.

20. Peter Zumthor, *Atmospheres: Architectural Environments/Surrounding Objects* (Basel, Boston, and Berlin: Birkhauser, 2006), 14.

21. Pablo Neruda, "Towards an Impure Poetry," in *Five Decades: Poems 1925-1970*, trans. Ben Belitt (New York: Grove Press, 1974), xxi.

CHAPTER THREE

1.   Anthony Synnott, "Puzzling over the Sense: From Plato to Marx," in *Varieties of Sensory Experience,* ed. David Howes (Toronto: University of Toronto Press, 1991), 63.

2.   Louis Sullivan, *Kindergarten Chats* (New York: Dover, 1979), 67.

3.   Montagu, *Touching,* xiii.

4.   James J. Gibson, *The Senses Considered as Perceptual Systems* (Westport, CT: Greenwood Press, 1966), 4.

5.   James J. Gibson, *The Ecological Approach of Visual Perception* (Boston: Houghton Mifflin, 1979), 143.

6.   Charles Darwin, *On the Origin of Species* (New York: D. Appleton and Company, 1882), 161.

7.   Ibid., 162.

8.   Gibson, *The Ecological Approach,* 143.

9.   Ibid., 126.

10. Merleau-Ponty, *The Visible and the Invisible*, 199.

11. Maurice Merleau-Ponty, "The Eye and the Mind," in ed. Thomas Baldwin, *Maurice Merleau-Ponty, Basic Writings* (London and New York: Routledge, 2004), 312.

12. Merleau-Ponty, *The Visible and the Invisible*, 132.

13. William James, "What is an Emotion?" in Carl George Land and William James, *Emotions* (New York: Hafner Publishing Company, 1967), 13.

14. David Howes, "Introduction: To Summon All the Senses," in *Varieties of Sensory Experience*, 3.

15. Ibid., 4.

16. Constance Classen, "Two South American Cosmologies," in *Varieties of Sensory Experience*, 246.

17. Ian Ritchie, "The Senses in Hausaland," in *Varieties of Sensory Experience*, 194.

18. Paul Shepard, *The Only World We've Got* (San Francisco: Sierra Club Books, 1996), 3.

19. Michael Moore, *The Future of the Body* (New York: Tarchner/Putnam, 1992), 201.

20. Ibid., 201.

21. Gibson, *The Senses Considered*, 85.

22. Ibid., p. 83

23. Ibid., p. 89

24. *Soundscape* is a term coined by R. Murray Schafer.

5. As cited in "Amichai, Israel's Most Important and Influential Poet, Dies at 76," *The New York Times,* September 22, 2000.

6. As cited in Bachelard, *Poetics of Space*, xvii.

7. George Lakoff and Mark Johnson, *Metaphors We Live By* (Chicago: University of Chicago Press, 1981), 146. (All subsequent references will be to this edition.)

8. As cited in Mumford, *The Pentagon of Power*, 56.

9. Richard Dawkins, *The Blind Watchmaker* (New York: W.W. Norton, 1996), 4.

10. Le Corbusier, *Towards a New Architecture*, trans. Frederick Etchells (1927; New York: Praeger, 1974), 12.

11. Ibid., 210.

12. Ibid., 59.

13. Ibid., 20.

14. Merleau-Ponty, *The Visible and the Invisible*, 15. Victor Hugo, *Notre Dame de Paris*, 3.

15. Charles Jencks, *Architecture of the Jumping Universe* (London and New York: Academy Editions, 1995), 129.

16. Mumford, *Pentagon of Power*, 420.

17. Arnold Modell, *Imagination and the Meaningful Brain* (Cambridge, MA: MIT Press, 2006), 26.

18. Ibid., xii.

19. Marco Iacoboni, *Mirroring People: The Science of Empathy and How We Connect with Others* (New York: Ferrar, Strauss and Giroux, 2009), 17.

CHAPTER FIVE

1. Lao Tzu, *Tao Te Ching*, trans. Robert W. Dunne (Bloomington, IN: Author House, 2008), 43.

2. As cited in Guy Claxton, *Hare Brain, Tortoise Mind: Why Intelligence Increases When You Think Less* (London: Fourth Estate, 1997), 28.

3. Lancelot Law Whyte, *The Unconscious before Freud* (London: Julian Friedmann, 1978), 10.

4. William James, *The Varieties of Religious Experience: A Study of Human Nature* (London: Longmans Green & Co., 1911), 388.

5. Quoted in Guy Claxton, *The Wayward Mind* (London: Little, Brown, 2005), 204.

6. Linda Hogan, *Dwellings: A Spirtual History of the Living World* (New York: W. W. Norton, 1995), 88.

7. Bachelard, *The Poetics of Space*, xxxvi.

8. Georges Spyridaki, *Mort Lucide* (Paris: Seghers, 1953), 35.

9. Marcel Proust, *Remembrance of Things Past*, vol. I: *Swann's Way* (New York: Random House, 1992), 61.

10. As cited in David Howes. "Olfaction and Transition," in *Varieties of Sensory Experience,* 140.

11. Compared to other animals our olfactory sense is crude; the delicate monarch butterfly can smell her mate from two miles away.

12. *Peripersonal space* is a neurological term that refers to the space within an arm's length of one's body. Peripersonal space plays an important role in understanding tool use and varies widely among individuals and cultures.

13. Richard Serra, interview with Lynne Cook and Michael Govan, in *Richard Serra: Torqued Ellipses* (New York: DIA Center for the Arts, 1997), 27-8.

14. Walter Freeman, *How Brains Make up Their Minds* (New York: Columbia University Press, 2000), 32.

15. Michael Ondaatje, *The English Patient* (New York: Vintage, 1993), 261.

16. Susan Engel, *Context is Everything: The Nature of Memory* (San Francisco: W.H. Freeman, 2000), 4.

17. As cited in Juhani Pallasmaa, *Encounters: Architectural Essays*, ed. Peter MacKeith (Helsinki: Rakennustieto Publishing, 2008), 125.

18. Louis Gluck, *The Seven Ages* (New York: HarperCollins, 2002), 14.

19. Sullivan, *Kindergarten Chats*, 170.

20. Suzuki, *Zen and Japanese Culture*, 142-3.

21. As cited in Suzuki, *Zen and Japanese Culture*, 238.

CHAPTER SIX

1. As cited in *Second Nature*, exh. cat. (Tokyo: 21_21 Design Site Press, 2008), 67.

2. Russell N. Van Gelder, "Non-Visual Photoreception: Sensing Light Without Sight," *Current Biology* 18 (Jan. 2008): 38-9.

3.   Maurice Merleau-Ponty, *The Visible and the Invisible*, 213.

4.   Jun'ichiro Tanizaki, *In Praise of Shadows* (New Haven, CT: Leete's Island Books, 1977), 30.

5.   Ibid., 14.

6.   As cited in Maurice Merleau-Ponty, *The Visible and the Invisible*, 49.

7.   As cited in *The New York Times Book Review*, vol. 72 (1967): 61.

8.   Loren Eiseley, *The Mind as Nature* (New York: Harper & Row, 1962), 29.

9.   Paul Steinhardt and Neil Turok, *The Endless Universe* (New York: Doubleday, 2007), 38.

10. Ibid., 61.

11. Ibid., 244.

12. Renzo Piano, "Architecture Is," in ed. Joseph Luis Mateo and Florian Sauter, *Natural Metaphor: An Anthology of Essays on Architecture and Nature* (Barcelona and New York: Actar, 2007), 167.

13. As cited in Joyce Monice Malner and Frank Vodvarka, *Sensory Design* (Minneapolis: University Of Minnesota Press, 2004), 140.

14. Flora Samuel, "Awakening Place: Le Corbusier at La Sainte Baume," in ed. Sarah Menin, *Constructing Place: Mind and Matter* (New York: Routlege, 2003), 217.

15. Ibid., 226.

16. Peter Davey, interview with Peter Zumthor, "Zumthor the Shaman." *Architectural Review,* v. 205, n.1220 (October 1998): 68-74.

17. As quoted in Guy Claxton, *Wayward Mind*, 222.

CHAPTER SEVEN

1. Edward T. Hall, *The Dance of Life: The Other Dimension of Time* (Garden City: NJ: Anchor Press, 1983), 81.

2. As cited in David Abrams, *The Spell of the Sensuous* (New York: Vintage Books, 1997), 200.

3. As cited in Jorge Luis Borges, *Seven Nights*, trans. Eliot Weinberger (New York: New Directions Books, 1980), 115.

4. Hall, *The Dance of Life*, 118.

5. Linneuas proposed the "Flower Clock" in his *Philosophia Botanica* (1751).

6. Richard G. Stevens, "Artificial Lighting in the Industrialized World: Circadian Disruption and Breast Cancer," *Cancer Causes and Control* 17 (2006): 501-507.

7. Ibid., 502.

8. Ibid., 503.

9. John Dewey, *Art and Experience* (New York: Perigee, 1934), 150.

10. Merleau-Ponty, *The Visible and the Invisible*, 153.

11. Hall, *The Dance of Life,* 157.

12. Rasmussen, *Experiencing Architecture,* 136.

13. Schafer, *The Soundscape,* 78.

14. As cited in Hall, *The Dance of Life,* 163.

15. John Ruskin, as cited in Pallasmaa, "Hapticity and Time," 82.

16. As cited in Moore, *The Future of the Body,* 1.

17. Pallasmaa, "Hapticity and Time," 80.

18. As cited in Kerry S. Walters, *Soul Wilderness: A Desert Spirituality* (New York: Paulist Press, 2001), 90. M. Mostafavi and D. Leatherbarrow, *On Weathering: The Life of Buildings in Time* (Cambridge, MA: MIT Press, 1993).

19. Tanizaki, *In Praise of Shadows*, 11.

20. As cited in David Van Zanten, "Félix Duban and the Buildings of the Ecole des Beaux-Arts," *Journal of the Society of Architectural Historians*, (October 1978): 172, n. 35.

21. Andy Goldsworthy, *Time* (New York: Harry N. Abrams, 2000), 7.

22. Ibid., 8.

23. Merleau-Ponty, *The Visible and the Invisible*, 265.

24. Sullivan, *Kindergarten Chats*, 32.

25. Andrew Kudless (Lecture, SFMOMA, San Francisco, CA, November 2008).

26. Martin Heidegger, *Basic Writings*, 388.

27. Mary Oliver, "What is it?" in *House of Light* (Boston: Beacon Press, 1990), 26.

CHAPTER EIGHT

1. Vitruvius, *The Ten Books on Architecture*, trans. Morris H. Morgan (Cambridge, MA: Harvard University Press, 1914), 38.

2. Gaston Bachelard, *The Poetics of Reverie: Childhood, Language and the Cosmos*, trans. Daniel Russell (Boston: Beacon Press, 1969), 193.

3. Anna Antonopoulos, "The Double Meaning of Hestia: Gender, Spirituality and Signification in Antiquity," *Women and Language*, v. 16, n. 1 (1993).

4. Jean Pierre Vernant, *Myth and Thought Among the Greeks* (London: Routledge, 1983), 160.

5. Alberto Pérez-Gómez, "The Space of Architecture: Meaning as Presence and Representation," in Steven Holl, et. al, *Questions of Perception: Phenomenology of Architecture* (Tokyo and San Francisco: A + U and William Stout Publishers, 2008), 23.

6. Vernant, *Myth and Thought*, 160.

7. Rainer Maria Rilke, "Sonnets to Orpheus," in Anita Barrows and Joanna Macy, *A Year with Rilke* (New York: HarperCollins, 2009), 60.

8. Bachelard, *Poetics of Reverie*, 36.

9. Bachelard. *Psychoanalysis of Fire*, 14.

10. Ibid., 10.

11. Tom Driver, *The Magic of Ritual: Our Need for Liberating Rites that*

Transform Our Lives and Our Communities (San Francisco: HarperSan Francisco, 1993), 31.

12. Richard Wrangham, *Catching Fire: How Cooking Made Us Human* (New York: Basic Books, 2009), 83.

13. Bachelard, *Psychoanalysis of Fire*, 75.

14. Ibid., 74.

15. Ibid., 74.

16. As cited in Malner, *Sensory Design*, 184.

17. As cited in Sarah Menin and Flora Samuel, *Nature and Space: Aalto and Le Corbusier* (London: Routledge, 2003), 71.

18. Kosho Uchiyama, *Refining Your Life: From the Zen Kitchen to Enlightenment,* trans. Thomas Wright (New York: Weatherhill, 1987), 67.

19. Abraham Maslow, *Religions, Values and Peak Experiences* (New York: Penguin, 1964), x.

CHAPTER NINE

1. Bachelard, *The Poetics of Space,* xxxvi.

2. As cited in Reyner Banham, *Theory and Design in the First Machine Age,* (Cambridge, MA: MIT Press, 1960), 278.

3. Davey, "Zumthor the Shaman," 74.

4. Hall, *The Hidden Dimension*, 62.

5. Banham, *Theory and Design,* 283.

6. Rasmussen, *Experiencing Architecture,* 177.

7. Frank Wilson, *The Hand: How Its Use Shapes the Brain, Language, and Human Culture* (New York: Vintage Books, 1999), 37.

8. As quoted by Juhani Pallasmaa, *The Thinking Hand: Existential and Embodied Wisdom in Architecture* (West Sussex: John Wiley & Sons, 2009), 47.

9. Francoise de Franclieu and Architectural History Foundation, *Le Corbusier Sketchbooks, vol. 4: 1957-64* (Cambridge, MA: MIT Press, 1982).

10. Mumford, *The Pentagon of Power,* 422.

11. Nicolas Ray, *Alvar Aalto* (New Haven, CT: Yale University Press, 2005), 161.

12. Loren Eiseley, *The Mind as Nature* (New York: Harper & Row, 1962), 10.

13. As quoted in Giedion, *Time, Space, Architecture,* 28.

14. Charles Darwin, *The Autobiography of Charles Darwin, 1809-1882: With Original Omissions Restored*, ed. Nora Barlow (London: Collins, 1958), 139.

15. Sullivan, *Kindergarten Chats*, 198-9.

16. Ibid., 199.

17. Borges, *Seven Nights*, 93.

18. Suzuki, *Zen and Japanese Culture*,104-5, 109, 157.

19. Dewey, *Art and Experience*, 26-7.

CHAPTER TEN

1. Nicholas Carr, "Is Google Making Us Stupid? What the Internet is Doing to Our Brains," in *The Atlantic* (July/August 2008).

2. William James, *The Principles of Psychology* (New York: Henry Holt and Company, 1890), 403-4.

3. B. Alan Wallace, *The Attention Revolution: Unlocking the Power of the Focused Mind* (Somerville, MA: Wisdom Publications, 2006), 3.

4. John Dewey, *Experience and Nature* (New York: Dover, 1958), 234.

5. As cited in "City Life and the Brain," in *The Harvard Mahoney Neuroscience Institute Letter*, vol. 16, no. 3 (Fall 2010): 1-3.

6. Steven Holl, "Questions of Perception—Phenomenlogy of Architecture," in *Questions of Perception,* 40.

7. Peter Zumthor, *Thinking Architecture*, 31.

8. Alberto Pérez-Gómez, *Built Upon Love: Architectural Longing after Ethics and Aesthetics* (Cambridge, MA: MIT Press, 2008), 204.

9. Edward T. Hall, *The Dance of Life*, 153.

10. Pérez-Gómez, *Built upon Love*, 204.

11. Ibid., 5.

12. Hall, *The Dance of Life*, 152.

13. Ibid., 152.

14. Uchiyama, *Refining your Life*, 54.

15. Bernard Leach, *Hamada, Potter* (New York: Kodansha International 1975), 135-6.

16. As cited in Plinio Prioreschi, *A History of Medicine, vol. 3, Roman Medicine* (Omaha, NE: Horatio Press, 1998), 278.

17. Robert McCarter, *Louis I. Kahn* (London: Phaidon, 2005), 463.

18. As cited in Leonard Sweet, *Nudge: Awakening Each Other to the God Who is Already There* (Colorado Springs, CO: David C. Cook, 2010), 51.

CHAPTER ELEVEN

1. Merleau-Ponty, *Phenomenology of Perception*, 332

2. Arnold Berleant and Allen Carlson, ed., *The Aesthetics of Human Environments* (Peterborough, ON: Broadview Press, 2006).

3. Walter, *Placeways*, 121.

4. Plato, *Timaeus*, trans. Benjamin Jowett (New York: Scribner & Armstrong, 1873), 49a.

5. As cited in Edward Casey, *The Fate of Place: A Philosophical History* (Berkeley and London: University of California Press, 1998), 339.

6. Pérez-Gómez, *Built upon Love*, 46.

7. Walter, *Placeways*, 204.

8. Vincent Scully, *The Earth, the Temple and the Gods: Greek Sacred Architecture* (New York: Praeger, 1969), 214.

9. Bruce Brooks Pfeiffer, *Frank Lloyd Wright Selected Houses* 3 (Tokyo: A.D.A. Edita, 1989), 22.

10. Hogan, *Dwellings*, 41.

11. Merleau-Ponty, *The Visible and the Invisible*, 118.

12. Walter, *Placeways*, 211.

13. Pérez-Gómez, *Built upon Love*, 204.

14. Rainer Marie Rilke, *Duino Elegies,* ed. J.B. Leishman and Stephen Spender (New York: Norton, 1963), 77.

CHAPTER TWELVE

"To Dwell in Possibility" is borrowed from Emily Dickinson's poem by the same title.

1. Robert Sabatier, *Dedicace d'un Navire*, as cited in Bachelard, *Poetics of Reverie*, 171.

2. Hogan, *Dwellings*, 123-4.

3 As cited in Cook and Govan, in *Richard Serra,* 27-8.

4. Merleau-Ponty, *The Visible and the Invisible*, 139.

IMAGE CREDITS

Cover photo by Richard Barnes, *Refuge*. Courtesy of Richard Barnes.

Page 11   Pieter Brueghel, *The Fall of Icarus*, 1588. Museum of Fine Arts, Brussels. Courtesy of Art Resource, New York, NY.

Page 22   Steven Holl Architects, Herning Museum of Contemporary Art, Herning, Denmark. Photo by Thomas Moelvig. Courtesy of Steven Holl.

Page 46   Oskar Schlemmer, *Figur und Raumlineatur/Figure and Space-Delineation*, 1924. Courtesy of Oskar Schlemmer Secretariat und Archiv.

Page 47   *Chichen Itza*, Mexico. Photo by the author.

Page 50   David T. Pang, *Paving in Prague*. Courtesy of David T. Pang.

Page 52   Steven Holl Architects, Herning Museum of Contemporary Art, Herning, Denmark. Photo by Thomas Moelvig. Courtesy of Steven Holl.

Page 54   *Teahouse at Shoren-in Temple, Kyoto*. Photo by the author.

Page 72   SANAA, *21st Century Art Museum*, Kanazawa City, Ishikawa, Japan. Photo by Michele Nastasi (Milan, Italy).

Page 73   *Mangrove in Belize*, Photo by the author.

Page 75   Tenzo Kendo and Transsolar, *Cloudscape*, Venice Biennale, 2010 Photo by Tenzo Kendo.

Page 77   Richard Serra, *Torqued Ellipses,* Photo courtesy of Richard Serra.

Page 82   Rick Joy Architect, *Catalina House* (interior wall). Photo by Bill Timmerman. Courtesy Rick Joy.

Page 82   Painting based on David Brewster's theory of light intensities relative to color cone lengths. By the author.

Page 89   Le Corbusier, *Cross Section of Sainte Baume*. Permission courtesy of Le Fondation Corbusier/Artist's Rights Society (New York, NY).

Page 98   Andrew Kudless, *P_Wall*, 2006. SFMOMA permanent collection. Photo courtesy of Andrew Kudless.

Page 103   Michael Van Valkenburgh, *Krakow Ice Garden* (detail). Courtesy of Michael Van Valkenburgh.

Page 104   Michael Van Valkenburgh, *Krakow Ice Garden* (detail). Courtesy of Michael Van Valkenburgh.

Page 107   Andrew Kudless, *Weathered P_Wall*, 2006. Courtesy of Andrew Kudless.

Page 108   Andrew Kudless, *P_Wall* (detail), 2006. SFMOMA permanent collection. Courtesy of Andrew Kudless.

Page 125   Le Corbusier, *Sketch of Sainte Baume*, Courtesy of Le Fondation Corbusier/Artist's Rights Society (New York, NY).

Page 138   *Taliesin West*. Photo by Pedro Guerrero.

Page 148   Wallace Cunningham, *Harmony House*. Courtesy of Wallace Cunningham.

PERMISSIONS

The author and publisher wish to gratefully acknowledge the permissions granted to reprint the following work:

"Of Havens" from May Sarton, *A Private Mythology: Poems* (New York: Norton, 1996). © May Sarton and W. W. Norton 1966. Used by permission of W. W. Norton.

Excerpt from "Towards an Impure Poetry" as it appears in *Five Decades: Poems 1925-1970* by Pablo Neruda, copyright © 1974 by Grove Press, Inc. Used by permission of Grove/Atlantic, Inc.

"Du Dunkelheit aus der.../You darkness, of whom..." from *Rilke's Book of Hours: Love Poems to God,* trans. Anita Barrows and Joanna Macy (New York: Riverhead Books, 1996). © Anita Barrows and Joanna Macy 1996. Used by permission of Riverhead Books, an imprint of Penguin Group (USA).

D.T. Suzuki, *Zen and Japanese Culture* (Princeton, NJ: Princeton University Press, 1959). © Bollingen Foundation 1959. Used by permission of Princeton University Press.

Linda Hogan, *Dwellings: A Spiritual History of the Living World* (New York: W. W. Norton, 1995). © Linda Hogan 1995. Used by permission of W.W. Norton & Company, New York, NY.